How to Start and Operate Your Own Design Firm

How to Start and Operate Your Own Design Firm

Albert W. Rubeling, Jr., FAIA

McGraw-Hill, Inc.

New York   San Francisco   Washington, D.C.   Auckland   Bogotá
Caracas   Lisbon   London   Madrid   Mexico City   Milan
Montreal   New Delhi   San Juan   Singapore
Sydney   Tokyo   Toronto

Library of Congress Cataloging-in-Publication Data

Rubeling, Albert W., Jr.
   How to start and operate your own design firm / Albert W. Rubeling, Jr.
      p.   cm.
   Includes bibliographical references.
   ISBN 0-07-054222-8
   1. Architectural practice—United States—Management.   2. Architectural services
marketing—United States.   I. Title.
NA1996.R83   1993
720'.68'8—dc20   93-27503
                                                                                            CIP

   3 4 5 6 7 8 9 0   DOC/DOC   9 9 8 7 6 5 4

ISBN 0-07-054222-8

*The sponsoring editor for this book was Joel E. Stein, the editing supervisor was
Caroline Levine, and the production supervisor was Donald F. Schmidt. It was set
in Palatino by PP&G, the compositor was Judith N. Olenick.*

Printed and bound by R. R. Donnelley & Sons Company.

This book is printed on recycled, acid-free paper
containing a minimum of 50% recycled deinked fiber.

To all those designers, willing to try

Contents

Preface

This book is about every designer's dream, starting and operating your own design firm.

Few attempt the journey. The tragedy is that many regret on a daily basis not having had the nerve to take the leap. Most do not attempt the journey because of the fear and risk involved. Some have numerous other concerns about the obstacles. Still others do not have a clue about how to start or run a business; all they know is how to design. This book is written to assist the majority of designers to make the decision. There is nothing worse for a person than looking back into the past and having regrets. One of the worst regrets one can have is "I wonder where I would be now if I had started my own firm five, ten, or twenty years ago?" This is precisely what motivated me in 1981 to start my firm. My wife and I saw an opportunity, looked the fear of failure in the eye, and decided, "So what if the new firm fails? There are other firms to work for." I did not want to be bitter for the rest of my life, always wondering "what if . . . ."

This book addresses directly those issues that prevent the majority of designers from creating a practice. It addresses the emotional as well as the intellectual challenges designers face once they have made the decision to make the leap and start their firm, with or without a parachute!

Many books are written about the intellectual issues, such as financial, banking, marketing, legal, and insurance considerations, and how to deal with them. And this is important because it is terrible to see so many designers start their firms, with no knowledge of business, doomed for failure. It is like seeing lambs led to slaughter. But few are written about how to handle emotional issues such as fear, risk, guilt, and success—the issues that keep the majority of designers from taking the leap.

This book has been written based on my 12 years of experience starting and building my firm, each and every day. It is my hope that these pages will bring to life the many wonderful experiences as well as the difficult issues one will face, and articulate the actual experience of starting a design firm.

The audience for this book are students in professional practice courses seeking a perspective on what the business side of design is like, professional interns who are planning their future, and licensed professionals working for others, but who feel that they can do the job and design it better than where they now work. Further, this book can serve as an organizational tool for those designers who have already started their firms and either can't figure out what is going on or who need a guide to assist them in understanding where they have been and where they plan to go. Finally, it is also written for those who may have lost employment due to the weak economy and who feel that they have no other choice, and out of desperation, have started a practice.

Starting a new design practice is one of the most exhilarating experiences in one's lifetime. It requires nerve, risk-taking, and above all, self-confidence!

The table of contents is organized in such a way that Part One will help you make the decision on whether to jump or not; Part Two discusses the reality of starting the new practice and all the areas of consideration you will have to address. Part 3 will help you organize your thoughts and plans and face those emotional issues that you wake to every day: fear, risk, guilt, success, and the future. Finally, the appendixes of the book include various glossaries for reference when you discuss your new practice with accountants, lawyers, bankers, and insurance brokers.

Each chapter is introduced with quotations from many designers and other notable persons that relate to the topic at hand. These are real-life anecdotes that capture the essence and state of mind of those individuals who have been involved in the struggle. These statements bring to life the real and imagined fear, the hope, the happiness, and the reality of the human spirit in the daily saga of operating a design firm. I felt that adding this personal side would make this book less formal and prescriptive to the reader.

It is my hope that you will read this entire book to not only decide if you have what it takes to start a firm, but allow it to be your "silent partner," your comprehensive guide, reference book to aid you in your journey of success, once you have!

Albert W. Rubeling, Jr., FAIA

Acknowledgments

As with most authors, I am indebted to many.

The challenge of my life to date has been to maintain the critical balance among family, business career, and my professional activity with the American Institute of Architects. I have been able to maintain this balance (most of the time) because of the care and efforts of the following people:

The employees of Rubeling & Associates, Inc., Architecture + Interior Design, without whose efforts this book could not have been written. They are the individuals responsible for the day-to-day activity, survival, and success of the firm. Most importantly, I need to thank John J. DiMenna, AIA, for his unbelievable loyalty and belief in my vision over the past 10 years and for being the analytical, follow-up "doer" that he is. What I start and never finish, he does. Rubeling & Associates, Inc., has been our laboratory to study various business strategies. Much of the research I have conducted and learned from is the foundation of this book's content.

I am also indebted to Ms. Ann Stacy, Hon. AIA who, as the executive director of the Baltimore chapter of the American Institute of Architects, gave me the ability to see the overall big-picture benefits of being an active leader in a professional association. Through my travels with the AIA, attendance at conventions, and meeting and conversing with other design professionals, I have come to understand that we all face the same problems in business every day, day in and day out. She has made me believe that I am a leader, and need to relay my vision and message to the design community.

Finally, I am indebted to my wife, Denise, and my three sons, Kyle Patrick, Korey Brown, and Kolby Albert. They have been loving, understanding companions in the roller coaster ride of my practice over the past twelve years! I thank Denise for believing in me and for allowing me to strive for my vision in life. I want to thank my sons for putting up with my leadership activities with numerous community groups and the AIA since those activities do not always allow me to be home for dinner every night or coach every baseball and lacrosse game. My family has been a constant factor in my success.

How to Start
and Operate
Your Own
Design Firm

PART 1

Making the Decision

1

So You Want to Start Your Own Design Firm?

I can remember the first year in business, it was the most romantic time in my design career. My wife was working, we didn't have kids or a mortgage, and all I had to do was worry about myself and my firm. No employees, no payroll. I just lived day to day with my simple practice, having to answer only to my clients and my conscience.

That first year in business was great. It was so simple, I did everything: design, draft, write specifications, write proposals, calculate my time sheet and translate it into an invoice. I typed all the letters and invoices on a typewriter, answered the telephone, balanced the checkbook, set up the accounting system, wrote off my first business expense, and received my first check for payment for architectural services rendered. God, it was great!

I remember answering the telephone for the first time with my new firm's name. Boy was it awkward. But it was a very proud moment.

Congratulations

This is the most exciting time in your design career. For one or more reasons, you know (or think you know) that you want to have your own design firm, with your name on the door—a place where you control the design decisions, where you work with the clients, and where you get the credit, reward, and satisfaction of making it on your own!

This book has been written as a guide and resource to the many designers who are considering starting, or have already started, their own firm. For some, this is a lifelong dream. For others, unforeseen circumstances—an untimely job loss or a host of other economic or personal reasons—have propelled them to strike out on their own. The intention of this book is to outline the magnitude and variety of business and personal issues that you will face in starting your own firm. The topics are introduced as considerations to address before, during, and after you establish your business. Not all can be dealt with prior to starting. However, if you have started, treat this book as your silent partner—and address those issues that you haven't, immediately! The book has many helpful checklists and glossaries for your daily use.

As designers, we have all invested many years in our education and in our internship, training to become licensed practitioners. Many of us have spent 10, 15, maybe 20 to 25 years working in a firm or numerous design firms. We know how to design, we have the knowledge of the building codes, we know how to put a project together. We love our work. But as designers, have we been trained for business?

Is a Design Practice a Business?

A *practice* is the carrying on or exercise of a profession or occupation as a way of life, whereas a *business* is a commercial or mercantile activity customarily engaged in as a means of livelihood. This is a very important issue that you as a designer will struggle with day in and day out for the entire time that you own your firm. Your attitudes on this issue will change daily. For years in design school, we were taught that design is a way of life. We ate, slept, and drank design. When we start a business and amass client responsibilities, accountability, and debt, we quickly become engaged in earning a livelihood! As design firm owners, we are accountable for more than just good design. We are also responsible for deadlines, code issues, public life, welfare, health, and safety as well as paychecks, benefits, rent, telephone bills, liability insurance, utility bills—the list goes on and on. The challenge of operating a successful design firm is maintaining a balance between design practice and design business principles. There may be times when design concerns must become secondary in order for a business to succeed.

Running a business (design firm) can provide some of the most rewarding accomplishments and some of the most gut-wrenching setbacks that you will ever experience. Business is life! You cannot truly appreciate the good without experiencing and understanding the bad. You will take your business to bed with you every evening, and wake up with it every morning!

Designing a new firm will require many long, hard, devoted hours in the beginning. Like designing a building or a bridge, it requires high creative energy and dedication to purpose. Starting a firm is just the beginning of a journey which will require constant attention to detail, maintenance, and course corrections—until the day you retire, sell, or "close down the shop." Investing time in a future firm's development requires persistence, stamina, and being up for it every morning! Few people possess all these qualities at once. That is why partners were created!

As an individual, you may feel that you are inadequate, that you do not have every trait that it takes to start and operate a design firm. You're not alone. The majority of start-up firms begin with two or more designers as partners, creating the firm because they share a vision and collectively possess the variety of traits necessary to succeed. Many feel the need to share the risk with others. That's okay—it's a natural human trait. In the ideal partnership, each partner complements the other in his or her particular strengths and weaknesses.

Can You Beat the Odds?

Whether you go it alone or with a partner, you face extremely challenging odds. Every year, over 1000 design firms start up in the United States. Of those, 800 survive the first year, 600 get past the second, and only 500 are left at the end of the third. After the end of the fifth year, only 250 of the original start-up firms exist in some way or form.

Summary

To own and manage your own design firm is one of the greatest and most satisfying challenges you can experience. You'll need sheer determination and an insatiable desire to succeed. Survival depends on success. The toll on personal health and family life can be very dramatic.

Now, considering all of the above, do you have "what it takes" to start your own architectural firm? How do you prepare for the journey? What are the important considerations to address before making the decision? (If you have made the decision to start, or have already started your firm, you will have already addressed many of the topics about to be discussed. However, let the book help you organize your thoughts and help you address the issues that you haven't dealt with, or even readdress those that you have encountered.)

Let's look at what it takes to make the decision to start your firm.

2
Facing the
Hard Questions

The president of my old firm was my mentor, and he died prematurely of cancer. It was an old-line firm, and the other principals thought I was full of too much piss and vinegar. When my mentor died, every rung in my ladder to the top was neatly sawed to prevent me from obtaining my ambitions to succeed in the firm. I was tired of always having to prove myself to the other principals, and I sure as hell wasn't going to prove myself to principals of another firm. I was running projects and proving myself to the firm's clients, and I felt that I only had to prove myself to me and to clients. That made me decide to leave and start my own firm, and not to work for another firm.

You know, when I used to work for the old firm, there was someone responsible for everything. There was the business manager who was responsible for billing the clients, getting the money in, and handing out the paychecks. The marketing guy sold the firm's experience and brought the new work in. The eldest partner was the patriarch of the firm. His stature as figurehead gave all of us confidence in our abilities to perform. Now I am all alone, and I have to do all of those things! And you know what? It sure is lonely at the top! I can't turn to anyone else but myself on all the decisions. The buck stops all the time with me. On one hand, it is really scary, and on the other, I wouldn't have it any other way because I know that I can handle it, and I know that I will get the job done because I believe in myself.

Making the decision to start your own firm can be one of the easiest or one of the most difficult choices you will make in a lifetime. For some of us, the decision is made by others, or by opportunities that present themselves. For others, it is strictly a personal choice: They simply "jump out of the airplane" and try a start-up, hoping their parachute will open.

The first question you must ask yourself is: "Why should I start my own firm?"

Why Do *You* Want to Start a Design Firm?

Are you unhappy with your current employer?

Are you dissatisfied with how your current firm practices design?

Do you feel that you can design better than the firm at which you currently work?

Is having your own firm a lifelong dream?

Do your in-laws need a design for a new vacation home in the islands?

Does your brother-in-law need a design for his new restaurant?

Have any of the firm's clients that you have worked with as project designer approached you for their next deal?

Can you and your studio colleague set the world on fire and show those stodgy principals in your firm who is better?

Are you, heaven forbid, driven by money, and convinced that you can make more by having your own firm than by working for others?

Are you tired of having to prove yourself to the unappreciative principals in your current firm?

Did you attempt to start a firm in the past and fail to get off the ground? You learned a great deal, and you want to try again!

You need to come to terms with yourself as soon as possible on these issues. Accept the answers and use them as a "driving force" on your journey to success. Making the decision to start a firm is very serious, but it is not life threatening! Once you have committed yourself, you can be certain that the road ahead will be long, winding, tumultuous on occasion, and blocked by obstacles. If your new firm fails (and that could happen), it not only may wreak havoc with your personal savings and other assets, but may also deal a blow to your ego.

As stated in the first chapter, many designers fail in their first start-ups, but the important issue is to learn from the experience. Founding a design firm is not for everyone, thank heavens. If so, there would be millions of sole proprietors, and who would get the large design projects? In this life there are followers, and there are leaders. *You need to decide which one you are.*

Working for someone else offers many advantages:

You have regular hours, with occasional overtime to meet an important deadline.

Your evenings and weekends remain free for family, friends, and hobbies.

You can expect to receive occasional pay increases over the years.

Your personal savings and assets are not at risk in the business.

You also need to weigh the drawbacks of running a business:

You will need to perform tasks and chores that you used to delegate and that you dislike or actually abhor.

You will not escape being "boss free." Your clients and suppliers will become your new bosses.

Your new firm will consume just about all your time and energy.

You will have little time to spare for family, friends, or hobbies.

Now ask yourself the crucial question: "What characteristics do I need to make it on my own?"

Entrepreneurs

First, and foremost, you or your partner should be an *entrepreneur* or have the entrepreneurial spirit. What is an entrepreneur? An entrepreneur is a person who organizes and manages any enterprise, especially a business, usually with considerable initiative and risk.

Some of the reasons that entrepreneur designers start their own firms are

Independence, a strong desire to be their own boss

A desire for recognition, prestige, and fame

An opportunity to earn far more than they could working for others

The discovery of an opportunity that others have missed or ignored

The challenge to compete against their former employer

Starting a firm will have a major impact on spouse and family or significant other. Being married to an entrepreneur is difficult, especially if you do not share the same instincts as your spouse. It is hard for a spouse to understand what motivates a designer to start his or her own firm. How can someone give up job security and take on what appears to be unacceptable risks? What will the spouse get in return? Long hours and dedicated hard work, with no guarantees. It borders on the irrational!

Nevertheless, the entrepreneurial spirit is incredibly strong. It is very difficult to talk someone out of it. The motivations are complex and differ from one person to another. In addition to drive, willingness to take chances, and persistence, the personal qualities shown in Chart 1 characterize an entrepreneur.

The entrepreneur *is* the business (firm) and is usually its founder, its motivation, and its force. Do you have any of the qualities outlined in the

---

CHART 1
Personal qualities of an Entrepreneur

Adaptable	Imaginative
Bold	Impassioned
Confident	Independent
Considerate of others	Innovative
Diplomatic	Inquisitive
Disciplined	Motivated
Energetic	Self-controlled
Ethical	Sociable
Flexible	Tactful
Healthy	Timely

CHART 2
Questions to Answer to Help You Make the Decision

What do I want out of life?

What are my aspirations, and are they attainable?

Am I prepared to work hard and make sacrifices?

Am I a self-starter?

Do I have common sense?

Am I in good health?

Do I have enough experience?

Can I lead others?

Can I take responsibility?

Am I a good organizer?

Can I make decisions?

Do people trust what I say?

Do I have a vision?

Am I a "driver" or do I need a partner who is?

What kind of manager am I?

---

chart? They are some entrepreneurial characteristics that drive designers to start and operate their own firms.

"Successful" entrepreneurs are willing to work hard. They get along well with others. They have good communications skills. They know how to organize. They take pride in all that they do. They are self-starters. They welcome responsibility and are willing and able to make decisions.

So before you commit yourself to an extraordinary investment of time, energy, ego, and money, think about and answer the questions posed in Chart 2 above.

This short personal appraisal is by no means an evaluation of whether or not you are a qualified entrepreneur. It is simply a means of focusing on your personal attributes and will help you decide on taking that major step. However, you may want to ask your close friends and/or colleagues to evaluate you so that you can get a more objective review. A word of warning: Do not ask your spouse or significant other to evaluate you. He or she will be more emotional than intellectual, and will give a highly subjective review.

Why Do Designers Want to Start a Firm with a Partner?

Many designers feel the need to share the day-to-day issues in starting and operating their new firm. Either they do not feel qualified to do it alone or they cannot bear the thought of assuming all the risk themselves. Others are presented opportunities, such as these:

> My studio colleague and I were laid off on the same day. We've both been moonlighting on residential projects, so we decided to help each other out and form a trial partnership over the next two months. What do we have to lose?

> My colleague, who left his firm a year ago, just landed a large project, and wants me to leave my secure position and help him out. He wants me to join him now, and become a partner in a few months.

Do you recall the question in Chap. 1 under Why Do *You* Want to Start a Design Firm? You need to ask those very questions of your potential partner. Developing a partnership with another is very similar to marriage. It requires an understanding of each other, the development of a commitment, in sickness and in health, for richer or for poorer. Does this sound familiar? Partners are business spouses. Many marriages end in divorce, as do partnerships. Be careful. This is serious business, and you should level with your partner on all the issues. Use the Partner Sanity Tests (Charts 3 and 4) in this chapter to serve as a beginning point in your discussions with your partner(s). Have fun with this exercise! Have both or all of you considering partnership fill out the charts. Then sit down and take the time to discuss the results. You will be amazed how effective this exercise will be in flushing out any concerns and issues that the new entity will face in house. Be responsible! The discussion could last for hours or maybe a few days. But consider how important a first step it is in obtaining a successful journey. (If you have already formed a partnership and are in practice,

Chart 3
Partner Sanity Test 1
Awareness

Vision and Goals

What vision do I have for the future company?

What goals do I have as a designer?

What goals do I have as a businessperson?

Do my partner(s) share my vision and goals?

What if they don't?

What are my expectations of the new company?

What are my expectations of myself?

What are my expectations of my partner(s)?

Am I an entrepreneur? How about my partner(s)?

Administration

What is business administration?

Do I understand the business administration needs for the new firm?

Am I interested in doing some or all of the administration?

Do I expect my partner(s) to do it?

Am I weak in business administration because I have never been exposed to it?

If all of us are weak in this area, whom can we talk to?

Finance

Do I understand the financial requirements of a business?

Do my partner(s)?

Should we each put money up front in the firm? How much?

(Continued)

Do I understand how to spend money wisely?

Should I handle the checkbook and other records?

Do I expect my partner(s) to handle the records?

Do I understand the importance of cash in a business?

Am I willing to be the financial person, paying the bills and calling all the clients for our money?

Do I expect my partner(s) to do that?

Do I know how to establish fees? Hourly rates?

Do I understand overhead? Do my partner(s)?

Do I want to deal with the accountant and the IRS? Do my partner(s)?

Do I want to deal with bankers?

Do I understand financial statements? Income and profit and loss statements?

Do my partner(s)?

Marketing

What is marketing? Will I be doing it or my partner(s), or both?

What image do we want the firm to have?

What will the new firm's name be?

How are we going to market the firm?

What niche markets are we strong in?

What will be our service offerings?

Do I know how to write a proposal? Do my partner(s)?

Do I know how to sell to clients? Do my partner(s)?

Legal

Do I understand the legal considerations that face a new business? Do my partner(s)?

Will I or we select the lawyer?

What form of business am I comfortable with? My partner(s)?

Do I understand design and construction contracts? Will I write them or will my partner(s)?

Insurance

Do I understand what insurance is for?

Do I care?

Do I like dealing with insurance issues? Salespeople?

Will my partner(s) deal with insurance?

Office and Equipment

Where will our new firm be located? In my house or a partner's house? Downtown or in the suburbs?

Do I understand commercial leases? Do my partner(s)?

Do I understand computers? Do I like them? What are my expectations?

Will we have word processing, spreadsheets, CADD?

Will I be doing the work? Will my partner(s)?

Design (The Land Mine!)

Will I be the firm's designer? Will my partner(s)?

Who will control the designs?

What are our design goals as a firm?

Production/Bidding/Construction

Do I know how to do working drawings?

Do my partner(s)?

Do I know how to write specifications? Do my partner(s)?

Do I want to do production work or only design?

(Continued)

Do I understand building and fire codes? Do my partner(s) understand these codes?

Do I know how to bid a project and issue addenda?

What are my expectations? What do I expect of my partner(s)?

Will I do shop drawings? Will my partner(s)?

Will I handle construction administration on site and in the office? Will my partner(s)?

don't ignore this exercise. You can still benefit from its focus on awareness and personal strengths.)

Weighing the Advantages and Drawbacks of a Partnership

Chart 3, on awareness, will help you and your partner(s) document your expectations of yourself and of each other. After you discuss the results and learn more about yourselves, go on to Chart 4 to evaluate your strengths and weaknesses in the seven key categories listed. Compare your results with those of your partner(s). The results should pinpoint all the advantages and drawbacks you feel about having this/these partner(s). The results should also identify those problematic areas in which none of you have expertise, and which you may have to address or become knowledgeable about. This test should have an incredible emotional impact on you and your partner(s), helping you search out any hidden agendas or uncommunicated expectations.

What Characteristics Should My Partner Have So That We Will Make It on Our Own?

By going through the exercises in Charts 3 and 4, you and your partner(s) will have a written and oral record of the major topics that affect a business, including a partnership.

Believe it or not, most partnerships do not conduct any exercises like these. The partners assume, presume, or expect whatever of their partner(s). Most designers do not want to take the time to effectively communicate

Chart 4
Partner Sanity Test 2
Strengths and Weaknesses

Evaluate your strength and weaknesses in the following categories.

	Strengths	Weaknesses
Administration		
Finance		
Marketing		
Legal		
Insurance		
Design		
Production/Bidding/Construction		

their thoughts, expectations, and aspirations on business topics because they either are not organized or do not feel knowledgeable enough on the subjects. They just want to design and leave all those other tasks as "necessary evils" for a partner to deal with.

The major factor facing partner(s) in a design firm is ego. Designers may or may not be strong in business affairs, but most are confident that they are good or the best when it comes to design. This trait can wreak serious havoc in a partnership. Many attempt to temper the issue by making each partner responsible for his or her own client's design work, and then sharing responsibilities for the remaining day-to-day requirements of the firm. Others couldn't possibly operate that way! Talk it over with your potential partner(s).

If you take the time to go through the Partner Sanity Test, you will be light years ahead of the majority of partnerships in practice. It may be difficult to take the time and expose your raw feelings and nerves to your potential (or real) partner(s), but isn't it worth the few extra days? Half the battle is organizing the topics. The Partner Sanity Test does this for you. The rest is up to you.

Obviously, once you have completed the exercises, all the bases of practice should be covered. If not, at least they will be identified, and you and your partner(s) can discuss who can best handle them, either individually or jointly. Use the test results to discuss and assign who will be responsible for each activity, according to your documented strengths and weaknesses. In a successful partnership, each member's strengths and weaknesses complement the other's.

Also, as stated before, entrepreneurial vision is needed to lead the new firm. If neither one (or none) of you is an entrepreneur, you need to seriously consider the relationship. Is it possible for one of you to develop entrepreneurial skills? What if both (or all) of you are entrepreneurs? It will take effort to make sure that you stay out of each other's way. Is there enough room in one firm for so many chiefs? Talk it out. You will be much better off if you do so now rather than later—when the partnership fails and good people are trying to figure out what went wrong, and a lot of money is being spent on lawyers and attorneys.

Finally, these are the ultimate questions to ask about each of your potential partners:

Do I want to jump out of the plane with this person as my partner?

What happens if my partner's chute doesn't open? Will I help?

If my chute doesn't open, will my partner help?

Will my partner be around in good times and in bad, in sickness and in health, for richer and for poorer?

Summary

Once you have answered all the questions above truthfully to yourself and your partner(s), and you are confident that you and your partner(s) have what it takes to start a successful design firm, *do it!* Remember the saying "Nothing ventured, nothing gained." Be true to yourself. If you feel that you have what it takes to start a firm, and you let small worries get in your way, you may regret your indecision for the rest of your life.

How many unhappy friends and colleagues do you know who didn't take the registration exam or start their own firm because of fear, and ended up bitter and jealous of others who did attempt to succeed? Will you be able to live with yourself in the future always wondering "what if"? There will always be an excuse to not "jump out of the plane"! Timing, your health, your family, your spouse, your mortgage, the money—the list can go on and on and on, for as long as you want it to.

Few attempt to bypass the excuses and take the leap. Once you have made *the decision,* you need to focus on the start-up issues that lie ahead of you, out there, as you begin your new firm.

PART 2

The Reality of a Start

3

Investing
in Yourself

The buck stops here! I am responsible for everything that this firm produces. I design, I draft, I specify, I build models, I invoice, I write the proposal, I write contracts, I buy insurance, I answer the telephone, I work on the computer, I work late at night, I visit the job site, I program, I space-plan, I check requisitions, I check shop drawings, I market, I do everything! Since I do all these things, I must remember to wear the different hat that comes with each job to do. I can't charge the client the same hourly rate for drafting a detail as I do for designing or writing a specification section—that wouldn't be fair. One minute I can charge $95 per hour, and the next $25 per hour! How am I going to keep it all straight?

If I am going to be working 16 hours a day, and I have enough work to keep myself busy, when do I market for the next job? How can I do two things at once—draw at my desk and market? What is marketing anyway? How can I promote myself if I am at the office all day, or on a job site, or traveling all day? Where is the next project coming from?

I learned to type in high school. I can type about 45 words a minute. But you known what, I can type only so many letters and invoices and spec sections. I am an architect, but when I started my own firm I didn't have any money to pay for a secretary. My answering machine did a great job of handling the phone, but having to type all the specs on a project cut into the time available for my work. What I did was hire one of the secretaries from the old firm on a part-time basis in the evening and on weekends. She typed all my specs and agreed to get paid when I got paid. She did a great job, and we continued doing business that way for the next year!

You invested thousands of dollars and hours of blood, sweat, and tears in your design training and education. Countless hours were spent in design studio as you unwound countless rolls of bumwad in search of the greatest design solutions. Thousands more were devoted to studying the works of the masters, learning form, function, and style. That is the role of the design academic institutions.

But how much time did you spend learning about how a design firm operates? A design firm is a business. Most of us could have cared less in our professional practice classes during the last semester of design school. We felt that we learned design and history in five or six years, and would have the rest of our lives to deal with contracts, administration, finances, and marketing. In fact, that was a job for the principals in the firms that we would work for. We just wanted to get a job, hold onto it, get as much experience as possible to sit for the registration exam, and finally become licensed to practice.

Dealing with all these start-up issues sounds scary, doesn't it? When you think about it, however, running a business is similar to living life day to day. You learn something every day, and you must build upon it to gain more knowledge, wisdom, and experience. Some people find living life scary, and if you are one of them, do yourself a favor and don't start your own firm.

The reality of a start-up, as any designer who has founded his or her own firm will tell you, is that it takes a lot more nerve than brains! That's the truth. Jumping out of the airplane is only half the battle! The other half is mastering the air currents, landing safely, and getting up on your feet!

It is humanly impossible to deal with all the start-up issues at one time or in a limited time span. Come to think of it, many designers who have had their firms for over 10 years still haven't dealt with all the start-up issues! So how do you handle something that appears so formidable—starting a firm, dealing with the issues, and coping with success?

The secret in starting a firm and addressing the issues is to recognize the fact that business is a journey, not a destination.

If you think about it, you can't brush your teeth in the morning unless you wake up first. You can't drink a cup of coffee until you either make or buy a cup. The reality of a start-up is to recognize that there are many issues to address, that you must deal with them one at a time at the appropriate time, and *grow into the business*. Let success and growth help you through all the start-up issues. Be logical and let the business expand through a natural progression.

For example, if you are starting your firm alone, you certainly do not need to have a phone system with 32 lines, or a retirement plan designed for 15 employees, or a network of 10 personal computers. Nor do you need an expensive new company car or an office located on the top floor of the tallest building in town. Be sensible! Purchase what you absolutely need to get the job done. *And that's it!*

Remember, a start-up business is a major investment of time and money. One of the toughest issues to deal with is money, or the lack of it. When you start a firm, one thing is for sure: more money goes out then comes in! Just think about the equipment and accessories that your former employer had. You will need to purchase much the same over a period of time.

Forget salary for a while! The only way to develop success in a young start-up company is to constantly reinvest time, money, and profits. Just take home enough money to live on. Invest the rest into the firm, because it will be the best investment of your life. This is the single, most important unwritten rule shared by all true entrepreneurs.

If you invest your money in stocks or businesses other than your own, you have more confidence in those businesses than in your own.

Confidence says a lot about yourself and your abilities. True entrepreneurs feel that no one can achieve success better than they can in their own business.

Summary

The reality of starting your own firm is being ready for the roller coaster ride of your life! This is one of the most dynamic life decisions you can make. The novelty of having your name on that "shingle" is short-lived and only skin deep. The journey that you will take can be the most exasperating as well as exciting adventure imaginable. Your firm will become a way of life for you.

We turn next to the major considerations that you have to face in starting your new enterprise.

4

Vision and Goal Setting

My goal in the first year of business was to gross what my salary was at the old firm, which was $16,000. Well, when I did that in six months, I thought it was an aberration! At the end of the year, the company grossed $32,000, more than double!

Now that I have my own firm, I have the freedom to do as I please! I must answer only to my client and myself! I can develop my own schedule. Most people who never started their own business think that it is all easy, and that you can take time off at will, go places, and do as you please. The truth of the matter is that it is easy to enslave yourself to your firm. If you have any kind of work ethic, your conscience will take over, and you will feel guilty when you are not working! Be fair to yourself and don't worry about how others view you.

Vision

What is vision in life or business? Vision is a trait of an individual or group of people who have the ability to anticipate what will or may come to pass. Some refer to visionaries as dreamers, because they look to the future. A more appropriate word for vision is imagination. All of us have imagination. As designers, we were trained in design school or by our mentors to expand our minds to think about objects in three dimensions.

Having vision is one of the most powerful traits one can possess in business. Being able to imagine the future and develop a plan to obtain one's goals successfully is a powerful trait. As designers, we all can imagine the conceptual final product before we refine the design, over and over again. Usually, the final design may be a little different than the one that we originally imagined; however, usually it is 90 percent of our original thought.

Most designers have this inherent design vision characteristic. Many however cannot apply the same principles and techniques to business. For example, when asked of one architect, "where do you expect to be in five years with your practice?", the response was, "I don't know, I can't even predict tomorrow! I guess I'll know in five years!" Another architect who has some degree of visionary traits responded, "I hope to still be in business with a staff of ten, providing design services in the restaurant market niche and the hotel market niche. The firm will be located in the city in approximately 3000 square feet of office space, and I'll probably have another partner by then"

What is the difference between the two statements? The fact of the matter is that both have some factual basis. However, the first, while being apparently true, is very short-sighted and doesn't take into account possible opportunities and *hope*. The second statement, whether partially obtainable or totally wrong, establishes *hopes* for the individual or firm to strive for and obtain.

Vision is 20/20 only in hindsight! Looking ahead and predicting the future is difficult and challenging. But trying to imagine the rewards and obstacles you will encounter in the future is a fun part of the business game!

As designers, we are trained to "turn a client's vision into a reality." What you need to do as a businessperson is to harness your design vision abilities and focus them on business activity. You have the ability, the imagination. *So use it!*

What vision(s) do you think that you have? How about your partner(s)? Examine your vision(s). It is important that you or at least one partner have the ability to exercise business imagination. The fact of the matter is that vision, drive, and imagination are your road map to and through the future! Otherwise, you would wander aimlessly through each day! Imagination and vision set the course.

Take your dreams and visions, utilize your imagination, and develop strategies to obtain the goals, both personal and business, that you want out of life.

Goal Setting

It is important in life as well as business to set goals to obtain. Goals are basically targets to aim for in the journey to success. Every businessperson wants to be successful, but since each of us is different, we may set different goals to achieve our success.

It is just as easy to set good goals as bad ones. Good goals should be set not only for business but for personal and family matters as well. Here are some examples of good goals:

Exercise every day

Stop smoking cigarettes

Stay healthy

Provide the best education for the kids

Take a great family vacation

Plan an anniversary getaway to somewhere exotic

Eat breakfast every day

Have dinner with the family five out of seven evenings

Obtain a balance among business, family, and personal needs

Play golf or some other sport at least three times per month to help deal with stress

Get to bed early every evening

Arise at the same time every day

Develop good work habits

Address all those you encounter—friends, family, and clients—as if they had a sign around their neck saying, "Make me feel important!"

Bad goals essentially are targets established in a vacuum. Such goals lack focus and vision because the path to obtain them is not clear or well defined. An unfocused goal is not only difficult to obtain but also frustrating to attempt. Many designers establish vague goals in their careers, such as:

"My goal is to have my own practice, *someday*."

"I want to produce the most creative architecture in the area."

"Maybe I'll work for this firm for another year. After that I don't know. I'll work for another firm that will challenge me more and appreciate my design talent."

"I'll wait until the right opportunity hits, and bang, I'm out of this firm, on my own!"

Goals for Your Daily Routine—and Beyond

If you want to be successful in life and obtain happiness, you must learn to establish realistic, obtainable goals on a daily basis, with an overview of long-range goals that serve as your "vision" about yourself.

In your daily routine, it is important to establish small obtainable goals, sometimes referred to as "inchpebbles." Simple goals, to be obtained on a daily basis, may include not only waking up at 6 a.m. but getting out of bed at 6 a.m.! Simple goals in business may include starting your day consistently at 8 a.m., making two marketing cold calls per day, designing your projects in the morning when you are rested and fresh, and conducting administrative and marketing functions in the afternoon, when most of your clients are out of meetings and in their offices, available to communicate with. Long-range goals—"milestones"—in the journey of success—are visionary and need to be the sum of many "inchpebbles."

Remember, the definition of a work goal is an end that you strive to obtain. If you are the type of person who needs structure in your daily routine, you should read the many paperbacks on "minute manager" techniques. Challenge yourself! Set goals, both milestones and inchpebbles, and you will be amazed at how quickly you begin to work in an organized fashion, contain fear and risk, and start to realize your dreams!

Sample Daily Goals

Awake at 6 a.m.

Eat breakfast every day.

Arrive at the office at 8 a.m.

Manage time effectively: design in the morning, take lunch at noon, handle marketing an client contacts in the afternoon, and "administrate" in the evening.

Be billable (chargeable) to clients for six to eight hours per day.

Market at least one hour per day on average.

"Administrate" for the firm at least two hours per day on average.

Record daily activities accurately through a time management system.

Generate an average of $500 or_____per day in cash flow for the firm to operate.

Reflect at the end of the day: "What did I accomplish today? How does it relate to my overall goals?"

Sample Weekly Goals

Did I accomplish five marketing cold calls this week?

Did I put in the production time that I needed to make the deadlines?

Was I billable 40 hours this week? If not, why not? Next week?

Did I generate $2500 or _____ this week in cash flow for operations?

Have I kept aware of trends and competitive forces and their impact on the firm?

Sample Monthly Goals

20 marketing cold calls per month

30 new marketing leads per month

160 hours of billable time per month on average

40 hours of administration time per month on average

$_____ invoicing per month

$_____ expenses per month

$_____ profit per month

Sample Annual Goals

200 marketing cold calls per year

300 new marketing leads per year

2000 hours of billable time per year

400 hours of administration time per year

$_____ invoicing per year

$_____ expenses per year

$_____ profit per year

Monitoring Efforts and Results

An important part of setting goals and working to achieve them is to monitor your efforts in the process. With many goals, there will be a major difference between the effort exerted and the results achieved. Some goals are relatively simple to state but difficult to obtain. Conversely, others are simple to achieve but difficult to recognize. Be patient. Achieving daily goals is what the journey to success is all about. It will be frustrating at times, but the pursuit of your dreams will make life for you, your family, and your new business highly rewarding.

Remember to measure your results, not your effort. Keep score of the game in points, not in how many shots you took!

Summary

Goal setting is an ongoing exercise. As with the design process, you need to set the easy, obtainable goals first, to gain confidence and develop momentum. This will help you gain the confidence you need to tackle the more difficult, complex goals of life—whether they involve business, personal, or family issues.

Challenge yourself! Use your imagination. Set goals—both milestones and inchpebbles—toward your vision in business. Be careful. Don't set vague goals or too many goals. Record them in your mind *and* write them down. (Business and marketing plans are discussed in later chapters.) You are on your way to realizing your dreams!

5
Financial Considerations

My first year in business, I refused to have debt. I paid cash for everything! Boy, have times changed.

Having to retain the services of an accountant is scary. First of all, I truly do not understand what accountants do, and I do not know how to read financial statements. I know that I need an accountant because I do not know how or when to file my income taxes for my company. I hope that I'll make the right decision!

I don't invest in the stock market or in any other company but my own. I feel that if I did so, it would mean that I thought other companies were a better investment, that I didn't totally believe in myself or my company. I invest my profits and dollars back into my company and myself because they are the best investment that I can control.

Now that you are a bona fide candidate to start your own firm, you must face the primary issue that all business founders must deal with: money. "How much do I need to start? How much is it going to cost me to operate? Can I afford to start my own firm?"

As much as we all agree as designers that design and being of service are important, the lifeblood of the firm is *money*. Like it or not, we all need money to live. Some of us need more than others, but money is the way to measure success and to keep score in business. Baseball teams measure success in runs, football and basketball teams in points, businesses in dollars.

What Are Your Financial Needs?

The first challenge that you must address is how much money you need to live on each and every *month*, not in a given year. Does your spouse have an income? How much money do you spend each week? Don't just think that "I need a salary of $45,000 per year to live." If you do not know how much money you need, sit down and analyze your expenses and spending habits of last year, or review what happened to last month's paycheck(s). You will be surprised how you spend money. This primary step is crucial to help you diminish your business risk. However, it is important to understand that what you think your needs are and what they really are may be different. Starting a business requires sacrifices. You will be amazed at how successful you can be with little or no money if you plan your start-up correctly.

You need to approach your new venture with lots of careful thinking and sound planning if you want to succeed. Your capital requirements should be diligently formulated well in advance of taking the plunge. Use the checklist on financial needs in Chart 5 to get started.

How Much Money Do You Need to Invest to Get Started?

Why do some designers start with $2000, others with $10,000, and still others with $100,000? The answer lies in the direction, image, and amount of work that a new founder has and wants to develop.

You need initial capital to cover many of your start-up costs. After you decide what advice you need and what equipment to purchase and where you are going to practice, you can strategize and spend your initial investment dollars wisely. Why hire the largest law firm in the area to set

CHART 5
Financial Needs Checklist
Month of _____

Item	Actual	Proposed budget	Deviation
Housing			
Monthly payment			
Taxes			
Insurance			
Utilities			
Water			
Telephone			
Heat/air conditioning			
Electricity			
Clothing			
Yours			
Your spouse			
The kids			
Food			
Automobile			
Payment			
Gasoline			
Maintenance			
Insurance			
Credit			
Credit cards			
Installment loans			
Student loans			
Other			
Life insurance			
Education (family)			
Medical and dental			
Taxes			
Recreation			
Travel			
Donations (church/charity)			
Miscellaneous			
Investments/savings			
Totals			

up your organization if you have a friend or close associate who will do it for a very reasonable fee? Do you have to have an office in the high-rent district? Maybe working out of your home is right for you and your new firm. Will inexpensive business cards do the trick in the beginning rather than overwhelmingly expensive ones? Only you can answer these questions. The point here is to think before you act and spend that precious commodity of cash in the beginning.

Think this through very clearly and carefully. One of the most common causes of start-up failure is lack of capital. Chart 6 will help you identify some of the start-up expenses associated with a new design firm.

Sources of Capital

Where does start-up capital come from? All knowledgeable business consultants recommend that at least half if not all of your initial business investment should come from your own personal reserves. You may have to work for a while at that job that you do not like, but the fact is that if you invest your own dollars on the venture, you send a signal to bankers, accountants, lawyers, and clients that you believe in what you're doing. If you own your home or other real estate, there is the possibility of a home equity loan. Another source of capital may be the cash value amassed in a life insurance policy over the years. Some designers approach friends and/ or family for the initial investment. Only you know how real and practical this approach is. If you do borrow money from friends or family members, you should work out a payment schedule. Be prepared. They will have difficulty restraining themselves from getting involved in the operation of your firm. Banks will lend money to start-up firms on rare occasions. Most often, a bank is interested in offering funds for operating capital to businesses that have a track record. For your purposes, the bank's primary value will be for short-term loans for purchases of equipment and other assets. Remember, the amount of initial capital needed to start a design firm is not substantial. Think, and spend wisely.

Learn How to Spend Money

As stated earlier in this book, one of the most important goals in operating a business is to have more money coming in than going out. Controlling the cash flow of the business is part of controlling overhead.

CHART 6
Start-Up Costs Checklist

Expense	Estimated cost	Actual cost	Date to pay
Business license/permit(s)			
Professional license			
Business opening announcement			
Rental deposit on office (if not in home—two months' rent)			
Telephone installation/deposits (if not in home) Answering service			
Utility deposits (if not in home)			
Insurance Health General liability Professional liability Life Theft Disability			
Legal Initial consultation Form of business papers			
Accounting Initial consultation Formal resolution			
Professional association dues Local State National			
Initial business "brochure"			
Letterhead/business cards			
Equipment/furniture Computer hardware Computer software CADD Typewriter Drafting desk(s) Desk(s)			

(Continued)

CHART 6
Start-Up Costs Checklist

Expense	Estimated cost	Actual cost	Date to pay
Adding machine/calculator			
Lamps			
File cabinet(s)			
Flat file(s)			
Conference table			
Chair(s)			
Telephone			
Telephone answering machine			
Facsimile machine			
Car phone/pager			
Photocopying machine			
Diazo machine			
Coffee machine			
Library shelving			
Supplies			
Pens/pencils			
Markers			
Mylar			
Bumwad/tracing paper			
Vellum			
Drafting tape			
Paper clips			
Post-ups			
Legal pads			
Telephone message pads			
Computer disks			
Light bulbs			
Measuring tapes			
Camera			
Photocopy paper			
Fax paper			
Other/miscellaneous			
TOTAL			

Use common sense. Ask yourself: "Does this expenditure make sense?" Pass the decision by your "new business conscience" and ask: "Is this expenditure *good* for the business?"

If the answer to both questions is a truthful yes, then go ahead and spend the funds. However, remember it is easy to justify emotional needs for ego purposes. Intellectually, sometimes it is better to say no to that expensive letterhead or that high-priced rent. When you spend money for the company's benefit, think of it as spending money not for "you," but for someone else, maybe that "other you." Think twice.

Having a partner can be good and bad when it comes to making decisions to spend those precious dollars. A partner can be a valuable check-and-balance system. But serious conflicts can arise if you cannot agree on how, when, how much, or why your new company should spend money.

The easiest way to control the expenditure of money is to develop a preliminary operating budget. Budgeting will be easy at first, since your new firm will have relatively little overhead or accounts receivable. Just remember the golden rule: "Don't spend more than comes in."

The basic purpose of a preliminary budget is to identify your income and expenditures and establish a goal for profit. Achieving a profit is the fundamental challenge that all businesses in the free-enterprise system face. The budget that you set can be annual, monthly, weekly, or even daily. As your firm grows, budgeting will become more complex. But when it comes time to "cut the overhead," the budget will be a valuable tool in helping you understand your business operation and make "finding the fat" easier. An operating budget is just as important as any financial, legal, or design plan. Even when you are starting out, having a budget will help you measure your success and provide a roadmap to achieve your goals.

Chart 7 summarizes the major categories of monthly expenses that a design firm will encounter. Use it as a guideline to expand and refine as your new company grows!

Learn the Importance of Cash

When you start your firm, you may invest not only your money (or other people's money) into the venture but also those monies you will be receiving from your clients (accounts receivable). In business, it is very important to convert your accounts receivable into cash as quickly as possible. Why is that? The longer the money sits in your clients' pockets, the more expenses your firm will incur, and if the cash isn't there to pay the bills, stress sets in. You need money to pay for the operation of your company.

If the failure of design firms can be attributed to one major factor, it is the inability to manage accounts receivable. Remember the principals in your

CHART 7
Monthly Operating Expense Checklist

Expense	Estimated cost	Actual cost	Date to pay
Accounting/audit/tax			
Advertising			
Auto/gas/oil/repairs			
Auto registration/insurance			
Bank service charges			
Business entertainment			
CADD supplies			
Car payment			
Car phone			
Computer lease			
Computer repair services			
Computer loans			
Contributions			
Conventions			
Copier lease			
Equipment rental			
Federal unemployment tax			
General office brochure			
Health insurance			
Interest expenses			
Legal expenses			
Liability insurance			
Life insurance			
Miscellaneous licenses			
Bank loans			
Office supplies			
Other office expenses			
Payroll			
Payroll taxes			

Expense	Estimated cost	Actual cost	Date to pay
Photography			
Postage/shipping/delivery			
Professional development			
Pension plan and trust			
Public relations			
Rent			
Repairs/maintenance			
Retail sales tax			
State unemployment tax			
Temporary help			
Telephone			
Utilities			
Workers' compensation			
TOTAL			

(Continued)

old firm discussing clients who did not pay for 90, 120, even 180 days? Designers are such good scouts when it comes to asking for money for services rendered that they end up defeating themselves. Designers are so sensitive, they don't want to offend the client. They fail to understand that if they are slow in meeting their accounts payable, they may incur interest, which erodes the bottom line of profit of the firm. Further, they may get a bad credit rating. Designers are concerned about design, not the dirty M word (money).

Well, forget all that—starting now! *Money for operations is more important than design in running a business.* Blasphemy! you say. Think of it this way: Sure design is important and, yes, as a designer you are who and what you design. But if the money isn't there to pay the consultants, vendors, employees, Uncle Sam, and your own salary, *you will not remain in business very long.* You will not be able to produce the design masterpieces that only *you* can create and be remembered for!

Cash is king in business.

To be a successful designer, you must be able to afford and pay your expenses. To help manage your cash flow, you need to develop a "seventh" sense, a gut feeling about one vital sign of the business: the need for cash. This cash conscience will help you manage the business by knowing when to call clients for money to meet your need for cash (payroll, rent, insurance premiums, and so on).

How much operating cash does your business need? One rule of thumb is to take the average monthly budget for your new firm and divide it by 20 (the average number of business days in a month). The resulting figure is the "average" amount of cash that you should receive every business day.

Example.   Your monthly operating costs are $8000 (roughly a $96,000 to $100,000 per year business operation). You need to "average" $400 per day to operate. If you do not bill $8000 for the month, you are losing money. If you do invoice $8000 for the month, you will need to have approximately $400 per business day (or $2000 per week or $4000 every two weeks) arrive in the mail or be delivered personally by clients. Now, in real life, $400 checks do not arrive in the mail day in day out. Some days, no money will come in; other days, $2000 will be realized! Some weeks you may get little cash, and others you may get flooded! Get a sense of when your expenses are due, and anticipate your cash flow around them. It's better to call a client a week in advance to receive money rather than wait until a major account payable is due and interest is charged! Think about this vital sign—cash flow—on a daily basis. Anticipate cash and if it doesn't arrive, demand it! You are due the money; you earned it!

Many designers agree that it is difficult to collect on delinquent client accounts—never mind asking for interest on balances past due. But when it comes to the bank, or to credit cards, they readily accept the interest charges of their own creditors. It seems that designers have established a standard that all client receivables are slow, and they do nothing to improve the situation. If you and your client agree that you will be paid in 30 days, demand payment on the thirtieth day. Set some goals. After you send your invoice, don't just bury your head in the ground like an ostrich and expect a payment check in 30 days! Produce the invoice—present it in person if possible. If you mail it, allow three business days, and then call your client to inquire if it was received. Ask if there are any questions about it, any problems. Find out if you can expect payment according to the terms of your contract. It is much better to have this conversation now—and become aware of a potential cash shortfall because a client intends to pay in 45 days instead of 30—than to wait until the full 30 (or 45) days have passed! Don't be bashful. Believe it or not, clients will respect you for being conscientious about business concerns. It will further demonstrate your professional business skills and will cultivate clients with an understanding of their accountability and responsibility to you for services received.

Treat cash management with the same passion as design!

Establishing Fees

One of the most difficult issues to face and resolve in a start-up firm is how to "value" your services. What is your time worth to a client? Well, the answer to that question is *very* complicated.

When you worked for the firm that you interned with, you were probably exposed to the firm's billing rate structure, which on an hourly basis may have gone something like this:

Principal	$95
Project manager	$75
Project architect	$55
CADD technician	$45
Draftsperson	$30
Administrative secretary	$25

As an employee of the firm, you probably understood the rate differentials for various job classifications. A principal is of more economic value per hour than a draftsperson. But what may make you curious is: How did the firm develop these hourly rates? Did it use some magical formula? Did it find out what the competition charges and develop equal rates? And how come the firm paid you $18 per hour and billed your time at $55 per hour? What happened to the other $37? Did the principals "pocket the money"?

The answer to all these questions is that a business has *overhead,* or costs associated with operating the business. (We will look at overhead later in this chapter.)

When you start your own firm, theoretically your overhead will be less than that of your former employer. For one thing, you may not be drawing a significant salary or paying a high rent (or any rent if you work out of your home). You may not have an expensive letterhead, an expensive phone system, a company car, and so on. Therefore, the costs of running your new firm could and should be less than that of your former employer.

This fact suggests that your standard hourly rates should be less than those charged by your former firm. Rates? Did I say *rates?* Why would you set several rates if "you" are only one person? The fact of the matter is that in business, clients expect their consultants to be fair. Why should you charge clients $95 per hour to design or consult with them and then, when you return to your office, charge them the same $95 per hour to draft or prepare a specification? You must learn when you start your own firm that as the sole employee you need to wear many hats (or share them with a partner if you have one). Your value to a client is based upon which task you are performing. Use common sense! Why is a principal's hourly rate higher than a draftsperson's? Rate setting can be a frustrating exercise. However, to be successful, you must value your time differently for each task that you perform.

What Should My Average Hourly Rate Be?

The simplest way to determine an average hourly rate is to ask yourself "What was my salary at my former job?" and work from there. Let's look at a simple case.

Example.   Your employer is paying you $20 per hour in salary. There are 200 workdays in a given year (excluding weekends and holidays and two weeks for vacation, if you even take one). The 200 workdays equal 1600 prime billing hours, which translates into $36,000 annually. Now this assumes that you will be working 8 hours every workday on a project! Is that possible? The reality of it is that you will probably be working 12 to 16 hours per day and close to 300 days total in your first year! So the true translation is 3600 to 4800 hours! You will work this number of hours, first, because you will feel the need to and, second, because the risk of hiring another will appear immense. Therefore, you will accomplish the work of 2.25 people by yourself! Are you tired yet?

Whatever your former salary, or total number of hours worked, as your own boss you now have additional costs to consider. What other tasks did you perform, and what other expenses did you incur, in completing a project for a client? Did you rent space for an office, did you buy paper, did you use electrical energy, did you drive to the client's office or home and use gasoline, do you have any insurance, do you pay taxes? All these items swell the cost of doing business.

Again, when you start your new firm, your expenses should be minimal compared with those of other, established firms. Therefore, your hourly rate should be less. However, use common sense. If a client of your former employer asks you to do some work (does this sound familiar?), how much would you charge? To start with, you know what the market will bear. The client paid your former employer fees according to an approved hourly schedule. You could start off using the same rates. Some clients will pay those rates; others are more astute in business, understand overhead and opportunity, and expect or demand that your rates be significantly less! Know your market, understand the cost of running your business, and be fair. If you are lucky enough to have a client pay you the former firm's rates, you will be facing a very profitable project! Be smart and invest those profits in better equipment (computers, software, telephone equipment—anything to help make your job easier).

You will find that when you have to compete for a project against other firms, the price sometimes has an impact on the selection of a designer. Low-overhead firms with expertise will usually win!

Why do you think that in today's business climate all business-oriented firms are "right/down" sizing? *To control their overhead and become more competitive!* Sure it's tough to reduce staff and other business expenditures. However, lean overhead results in higher profits for a company. Higher profits can mean bonuses, new equipment, capital reserves, peace of mind, and much, much more.

Remember, when you think of what your time is worth, take into consideration the following:

What costs are associated with doing this project?
> My take home
>
> My expenses
>
> Targeted profit

What will the market bear?

Understand that you will have to wear many hats. *Be fair to yourself as well as the client!*

What is Overhead?

The principals of the firm that you worked for talked on and on about this "mystery term." You've heard it referred to as a number—perhaps two point five (2.5) or two point three (2.3). You've heard endless talk about cutting overhead. You've wondered why the firm multiplied your hourly rate by a factor and charged the clients two or three times as much for your work! How could the firm do that? Where did all the other money go?

In simple terms, overhead refers to all costs associated with operating a business. All costs! Therefore, the lower the operating costs of your new company, the higher your profit will be on every dollar that you bill. Every city has architectural firms that operate in "high design" offices and those that work out of "slummy" offices. We all know the impact of image. But if your clients never come to your office, why spend a million dollars on expensive furniture and rent? When you are starting your firm, the lowest rent that you can pay is to operate out of your own home—unless of course you get an offer of "free" rent from some other source.

Chart 8 is an overhead costs checklist summarizing the types of expenses a design firm can expect to encounter. The next exercise to perform is to calculate how much of your overhead is attributable to direct costs of a project and how much is indirect, not chargeable to a project. You will find that most of your direct costs fall into the following categories:

Auto mileage traveled to and from a project

CADD supplies directly attributable to a project

Office supplies directly attributable to a project

Payroll directly attributable to a project (normally 80 to 90 percent)

Postage/shipping/delivery directly attributable to a project

Photography directly attributable to a project

Telephone costs directly attributable to a project

Divide the direct costs into the indirect costs to find your firm's overhead factor:

$$\frac{\text{Indirect costs}}{\text{Direct costs}} = \text{Overhead factor}$$

Low overhead factors (ratios) are 1:1 or 1:2. Normal ratios for medium-sized firms are 1:4 to 1:6. Large firms have ratios of 1:5 to 1:75.

Let's return now to computing an "average" hourly rate to be charged by your new firm. First take your hourly salary rate of your current/former job and multiply it by the overhead factor to find your "payroll burden." Add the salary rate to that figure. Then multiply by a profit goal. The following example assumes an overhead rate of 1.3 and profit goals of 10, 15, and 20 percent:

Salary rate	×	Overhead rate	=	Payroll burden
$20/h		1.3		$26.00/h

Salary rate	+	Payroll burden	=	Salary + burden rate
$20.00/h		$26.00/h		$46.00/h

Salary + burden	×	Profit	=	Hourly rate
$46.00/h		(10%)1.1		$50.60
		(15%)1.15		$52.90
		(20%)1.2		$55.20

CHART 8
Overhead Costs Checklist

Expense	Monthly cost	Annual cost	Percent
Accounting/audit/tax			
Advertising			
Auto/gas/oil/repairs			
Auto registration/insurance			
Bank service charges			
Business entertainment			
CADD supplies			
Car payment			
Car phone			
Computer lease			
Computer repair services			
Computer loans			
Conventions			
Copier lease			
Equipment rental			
Federal unemployment			
General office brochure			
Health insurance			
Interest expense			
Legal expenses			
Liability insurance			
Life insurance			
Miscellaneous licenses			
Bank loans			
Office supplies			
Other office expenses			
Payroll			
Payroll taxes			
Postage/shipping/delivery			

(Continued)

Expense	Monthly cost	Annual cost	Percent
Professional development			
Pension plan and trust			
Public relations			
Contributions			
Rent			
Repairs/maintenance			
Photography			
Retail sales tax			
State unemployment tax			
Temporary help			
Telephone			
Utilities			
Worker's compensation			
TOTAL			

Remember that this figure represents an average rate only. You will charge clients more for certain tasks and less for others. Now think about what all these computations mean in real terms. If you have a profit goal of 20 percent, and thus an hourly rate of $55.20, and if you put in 4000 hours that first year, you will earn

$$\text{Hourly rate} \times \text{Hours} \times \text{Profit goal} = \text{Earnings}$$
$$\$55.20 \qquad 4000 \qquad .20 \qquad = \$44,160$$

A higher profit goal means higher earnings, of course—and you are your own boss!

Profit

Profit is the reason you are in business. Great design is why you are in practice. Profit is your reward for taking the many business risks and resultant stresses that affect you from ownership. The standard acceptable profit margin for government projects is 10 percent. However, this should not keep you from setting a goal of a higher amount.

Many designers do not understand what profit is. The way they perceive profit is that it is the money left over at the end of the year after all the bills are paid! If they have some profit that is fine, and if they don't, maybe next year will be a better one. How naive!

Profits in reality are monies left over after expenses. The strategy for a profitable design firm is to treat profit as an expense on a project. If your fee is $10,000 and you project a profit of $1500, then attack the scope of work and do the project for $8500. This will give you the profit you desire. Any time expended after $8500 worth of services erodes the profit figure.

Looking at the big picture, if you need money from a bank for equipment or a line of credit, the bank wants to deal with a profitable business, not one in the red. It wants to diminish its risk.

Profit is the final score in the game of business.

Be careful not to give work away! Many designers do not recognize the big picture. They take on a project for what they think is "at cost," without profit, and do not understand how they end up losing money. Many take on multiple commissions this way, and if they do not properly manage the projects, they will go bankrupt in only a short time.

Financial Records

When they start out on their own, most designers are likely to regard bookkeeping as cruel and unusual punishment. They will do anything to avoid doing it. They will get anyone to do the books. It appears to be such a tiring, thankless task that most designers would actually go without records if they could get away with it. Design can be so freewheeling, and accounting has to be so exact! All the numbers in a column must add up.

Remember, your financial records are a critical tool in tracking the health and profitability of your firm. Review them as "snapshots" of given moments in time to evaluate your firm's performance. Use the records as guides to make decisions for the firm. Acknowledgment of the records as tools will help you learn from the past, understand the present, and forecast the future. Your financial records can help you plan your investments, forecast growth, and keep tax liabilities to a minimum. They are the keys to your firm's success.

When you start your firm, whether you incorporate or not, arrange your bookkeeping in a simple manner. Open a separate bank account for your business. Believe it or not, many consultants operate their businesses out of their personal accounts to "keep things simple"! This makes life difficult in tracking and controlling business funds.

Document all your expenditures, no matter how large or small.

This is the first law of record keeping! Document expenses by using checks and credit cards for all your payments. If you pay cash, limit it to smaller purchases and *save the receipts!* If you cannot obtain a receipt, document the purchase in some manner. Some businesspeople carry a separate notebook to keep tabs on their expenditures in the beginning. You will be amazed at how quickly the money goes out! And you will learn that cash goes out from the company easier than into it! The secret to a successful business is to have more money come in than goes out. *That should be your first goal in accounting!* Your new firm is not the federal government. You can't print money or spend more than you can raise. Therefore, always remember to spend less than you make. Use common sense!

Bookkeeping

When you start your firm, have your spouse, a friend, or an accountant "set up your books" (establish your accounting record formats) and explain the fundamental rules of accounting. If you are proficient on a computer, buy a basic accounting software package to get yourself started. Remember, keep it simple!

You may not need a sophisticated five-part software package specifically geared to a design firm. Many a firm was founded starting out with a "one write" single handwritten entry system or a simple bookkeeping record for the first year in business. Remember, let the bookkeeping system grow with your company. Don't overbuy!

When you start out, if you enjoy working with figures, by all means keep the books for your company. This is the best possible training in the business world. It will help you better understand the day-to-day activities required to run a business. If you can't stand working with figures, consider hiring a part-time bookkeeper. Consult with your accountant for a recommendation—accountants and bookkeepers often work as teams.

Look for these traits in a bookkeeper:

A good bookkeeper understands payroll/general ledger/accounts payable/accounts receivable, not just one or two.

A good bookkeeper keeps track of every penny.

A good bookkeeper doesn't settle for anything less than 100 when tallying a column of figures.

A good bookkeeper can analyze figures, not just record them.

A good bookkeeper will keep your business matters private.

A good bookkeeper will let you know when your expenses are greater than your income!

Remember, when you start out, you may need a bookkeeper only one day a week or three days a month. The amount of time will depend on your work volume. Some designers keep their own books for the first year to "learn the system" so that when they do hire a part-time bookkeeper, no one understands the business and its records better than they do.

Do I Need an Accountant?

The simple answer to this question in business is *yes!* An accountant is one of four essential business team advisers. (The others are your lawyer, banker, and insurance broker.)

A bookkeeper is *not* an accountant. Your accountant will provide many essential consulting services when you start your firm. He or she will

Advise on organizational form (sole proprietorship vs. partnership, etc.)

Advise on tax considerations (IRS forms, payments, etc.)

Coordinate with your attorney

Determine whether to use a cash or accrual method for keeping your books

Select a bookkeeping system (one-write, computer, etc.)

Consult on preparing a business plan

Help introduce you to bankers and lending institutions

Prepare profit and loss statements

Prepare a balance sheet

Prepare financial statements

Advise on tax strategies and planning

You need to meet with your accountant for only a few hours a year, but remember to schedule meetings regularly, perhaps each business quarter, to update the accountant on your business plans, projected revenues, and methods of operation. Discuss the details of your operation: how much money you want to make or spend, cash flow, taxes, financing, and so on. Don't expect profound advice from your accountant if you get together only once a year.

View your accountant as an important person who cares about your business and your success. Share confidences; discuss your concerns and problems. Above all, be prepared for your meetings. Accountants are not inexpensive. Present your information in a precise, economical, thoughtful way. Don't give information haphazardly and expect the accountant to understand the data in one sitting! *Remember, accountants (bean counters) love organization and order.* Giving accountants information in a disorganized fashion will cost you more money in the long run.

Setting Up a Basic Accounting System

A designer, like any businessperson, must keep accurate and thorough financial records for all income received and expenses incurred. It is that simple! The purpose of financial records is to help produce income, control expenses, track cash flow, keep tax payments to the legal minimum, and comply with other regulatory requirements.

Accounting is the theory and *system* of setting up, maintaining, and auditing the books of a firm; it is also the *art* of analyzing the financial position and operating results of a business from a study of its sales, purchases, and other transactions. Your accountant will probably recommend one of the following systems to start your firm.

1. *Separate record keeping.*   As stated earlier, it is essential to separate your business books from your personal records, checkbook, and bank accounts. Financial statements will be easier to draft and financial applications will be simpler to execute. Most important, all business expenses will be traceable to one source. Personal draws are easily controlled and documented.

2. *Double-entry bookkeeping.*   Most accountants prefer the double-entry bookkeeping system for maintaining business records. Transactions are

entered first in a journal, then monthly totals of the transactions are posted to one of five ledger accounts:

Income
Expense
Assets
Liabilities
Net worth

Income and expense accounts are closed each year. Asset, liability, and net worth accounts are maintained on a permanent and continuing basis.

3. *Single-entry bookkeeping.* This system is not as complete as the double-entry method. It is simple and documents the flow of income and expense through a daily summary of cash receipts, a monthly summary of receipts, and a monthly disbursements journal such as a checkbook.

4. *One-write accounting system.* The one-write accounting system, through the use of a carbon or pressure-sensitive paper, posts a sales journal and monthly ledger. All your checkwriting is posted to the proper expense journal on the payables chart. You have a choice of using the system for payables, receivables, or both. It makes record keeping very easy for you and for your accountant. Think about using this system once you start writing about 40 checks per month. Many financial record companies distribute "their" version of the one-write system. Most systems are expandable to keep pace with your growth. Consult with your accountant, colleagues, or stationery store vendor to select the right system for your firm.

5. *Personal computer basic accounting software packages.* There are dozens of basic accounting software packages available to the small start-up business. Look for one that is adaptable for a design (service) consulting firm.

In the beginning, remember to keep it simple. Some packages will write all your checks, post the expenses, do payroll, and keep track of your receivables. As an extra bonus, they will produce trial balance sheets and income statements for your new enterprise! No matter how simple these packages may seem, before you purchase one (for as little as $39.95!), consult with other designers, ask your local AIA office if there is a users group nearby, and buy a software consumers report to compare. Learn from others and their mistakes!

Remember, your start-up capital is essential, important, and scarce.

Don't spend a lot on a worthless program that is out of tune with your new design practice. Take your time, and look for the right fit for your needs!

If you are not user-friendly with computers or accounting, think twice before you invest in software and a computer. Once you jump out of the airplane you'll have no time to teach yourself how to use a computer or software. It will eat up too much valuable time. If you think that you must have a computer and don't know how to use one, stay in the plane a little longer. Learn the system first, then jump!

Cash vs. Accrual Accounting

Record-keeping systems differ in their basic methods of recording as well as in the amount of detail shown. These methods refer to the rules for computing "taxable income" and, more specifically, to the timing of recognition of specific items of income and deductions in a business for the Internal Revenue Service (IRS). Whether your books are single or double entry, you must choose between two accepted accounting methods: cash or accrual.

Under the *cash* method of accounting, income is recorded when cash (checks, money orders, or currency) is received, and expenses are recorded when paid. The cash system shows only what you have received, not what you have earned. Many design firms prefer this method because it reflects the fact that they pay taxes on the receivables they have received rather than earned.

The *accrual* method of accounting records all income and expenses whether paid or not. This accounting system requires more bookkeeping effort than the cash method. However, most businesses prefer the accrual method because it provides a more accurate set of records of the firm. Bankers like businesses that use this method because it presents a "better picture" of the firm and its operation.

The Tax Reform Act of 1986 imposed strict limitations on the use of the cash method of accounting. Specifically, corporations and partnerships (other than S corporations and personal service corporations) must use the accrual method of accounting unless their average gross receipts for a three-year period do not exceed $5 million annually. Sole proprietorships, S corporations, and certain personal service corporations and partnerships may use the cash method of accounting. In practice, most companies continue to use the accounting method that appeared on their first tax return to the IRS.

The advantages and disadvantages of each system depend on your individual circumstances. Consult your accountant to assist you in making the correct choice.

Depreciation

Throughout your new firm's lifetime, you will have to purchase property and equipment from time to time. This property will usually last for several years, so it is not reasonable to consider the whole cost as an expense in any given one-year time frame. Therefore, when the property or equipment is purchased, it is recorded in your financial records as a fixed asset or plant asset.

The decrease in value over the life of the asset, known as depreciation, is treated as an expense distributed over the time period during which the asset is used. There are several methods of computing depreciation. When figuring depreciation, you should consider the following factors:

Cost of the asset

Its estimated useful life

Estimated salvage or trade-in value at the end of its useful life

The simplest and most common way of computing depreciation is the *straight line method*. Under this method, the estimated salvage value and any additional first-year depreciation taken are subtracted from the cost. The remainder is divided by the estimated useful life of the asset. The resulting figure is the amount to be charged off as depreciation each accounting period.

Example.   You purchase a PC for $5000. Its salvage value is $500, and its useful life is five years. If straight-line depreciation is utilized, the annual depreciation is computed as follows:

$$\frac{\$5000 - \$500}{5} = \$900$$

There are other methods of depreciation such as *sum of the years' digits* and *double declining balance*. You may choose different methods for different assets. For tax purposes, you must apply the same method to an asset over its useful life unless you obtain permission from the IRS.

Coordinate asset depreciation with the rest of your bookkeeping system. Let your accountant figure the method and record the data for your new firm.

Learn the Basic IRS Rules for Business

Why should you, a designer, learn the basic IRS rules? The answer is a simple one. If you want to be successful in business *and remain in business,* you must acknowledge the existence of the Internal Revenue Service. Uncle Sam wants to share in your success.

To the average person, tax law is a complex headache, a nightmare. That's why accountants were created, right? Well, leaving all your tax work, planning, and filing to your accountant is fine. However, you should know some of the basics. In design school you learned how calculus was the basis of structural calculations, and as a designer you needed to be exposed to the theory. However, in practice there are people called structural engineers who will handle all such challenges. Similarly, you need to depend on an accountant to do the right thing for your new firm.

Tax Laws

Many federal tax laws are designed solely to keep you from cheating Uncle Sam out of what he thinks is rightfully his: your company's money! Many other laws, however, are designed to save a company money by providing tax breaks. The IRS does make an effort to educate the public about taxes. But it is *your* responsibility as a taxpayer to investigate, understand, and file your taxes. Having a list of excuses for not filing on time is not good enough for the IRS.

One of the first books you should obtain prior to starting your firm is the *Tax Guide for Small Business* (Publication 334), which is free from any IRS office. It is well written, with updates every year, and contains thorough explanations of income, excise, and employment taxes for all forms of businesses: sole proprietors, partnerships, and corporations. You will also need the appropriate tax forms. A list is provided in Chart 9.

Accounting Period: Calendar Year vs. Fiscal Year

Every business must keep financial records and file appropriate tax returns for a given *taxable year,* which is either a calendar year or a fiscal year. A calendar year begins on January 1 and ends on December 31. Calendar year

Chart 9
Internal Revenue Service Forms

Sole proprietorship

Schedule C	(Form 1040) Profit or Loss from business (Sole Proprietorship)
Form 4562	Depreciation and Amortization
Schedule SE	(Form 1040) Self-Employment Tax
Form 4868	Automatic Extension of Time to File

Partnerships

Schedule SE	(Form 1040) Self-Employment Tax
Form 1065	U.S. Partnership Return of Income
Schedule K-1	Partner's Share of Income, Credits, Deductions, Etc.
Form 8736	Application for Automatic Extension of Time to File U.S. Return for a Partnership

Corporations

Regular "C"

Form 1099-DIV	Dividends and Distributions
Form 1120-A	U.S. Corporation Short-Form Income Tax Return
Form 1120	U.S. Corporation Income Tax Return
Form 1120-W (FY)	U.S. Corporation Fiscal Year Income Tax Return
Form 1120-X	Amended U.S. Corporation Income Tax Return
Form 8109	Federal Tax Deposit Coupon

Subchapter S

Form 1120-S	U.S. Income Tax Return for an S Corporation
Form 1128	Application to Adopt, Change, or Retain Tax Year
Schedule K-1	Shareholder's Share of Income, Credits, Deductions, Etc.

tax returns are due on April 15 (the fifteenth day of the fourth month following the end of the calendar year). Most small businesses use the calendar year—and the IRS prefers this format—because it is easier to contemplate. Most if not all of the IRS procedures are geared toward the calendar year. Chart 10 presents an annual tax calendar for calendar year businesses.

A fiscal year is a 12-month period ending on the last day of any month other than December. Fiscal year tax returns are due on the fifteenth day of the fourth month following the end of the fiscal year. There are strict, complex rules on who can conduct business on a fiscal year basis and when a decision must be made to adopt a fiscal year format.

Generally, sole proprietorships must use the same taxable years as that established by the founder/owner, which means the calendar year in the majority of cases. The same rule applies to partnerships, S corporations, and personal service corporations. However, the IRS will allow these forms of business to adopt a fiscal year format if there is a valid business reason for doing so. Regular corporations can choose either a calendar year or fiscal year format.

Why choose a fiscal year format? Some businesses have predictable annual cycles and find that coordinating their taxable year with those cycles better represents actual income and expenses for the business. Corporations often choose a fiscal year coinciding with their first month of operation in order to avoid a short-period tax return and extra taxes in the first year.

Again, discuss your options with your accountant *before* you start!

Who Must File Tax Returns?

A federal income tax return must be filed if annual gross income exceeds $5900 for a single person, $10,600 for a couple filing jointly, or $2300 for a married couple filing separately. (These figures may change annually. Consult a current tax guide.) Gross income means income before any business deductions. It is your total sales, fees, and commissions.

Every business must file a federal income tax return if net earnings from self-employment (business net profit) total $400 or more. (Business income minus expenses equals net profit.)

Types of Taxes

Income Taxes

The type of federal income tax return you are required to file will depend on the form of business you undertake. If you operate as an individual

Chart 10
Annual Tax Calendar for Calendar Year Businesses

January

15   Sole proprietor/partnership/S corp shareholder estimated tax due

31   FICA/FUTA taxes due

        W-2 forms to employees

        1099 forms to consultants

February

March

15   Corporation income tax due (calendar year)

        S Corporation income tax due (calendar year)

April

15   Sole proprietor income tax due

        Self-employment tax due

        Sole proprietor/partnership/S corp shareholder estimated tax due

        Annual return of partnership income tax due

30   FICA/FUTA taxes due

May

June

15   Sole proprietor/partnership/S corp shareholder estimated tax due

July

31   FICA/FUTA taxes due

(Continued)

August

September

15   Sole proprietor/partnership/S corp shareholder estimated tax due

October

31   FICA/FUTA taxes due

November

December

---

proprietorship (you are the sole owner and the business is not incorporated), you must report your business operations on Schedule C and attach it to Form 1040, your individual tax return.

If you operate as a partnership, the business must file a Form 1065. The partnership is not liable for federal income tax. However, the partners must report their share of profits or losses on their individual Form 1040.

If you operate as a corporation, the corporation must file a Form 1120 and pay taxes on the taxable income reported. If you receive any salary or dividends from the corporation, you must report them on your individual Form 1040. Gross dividends of over $400 must be listed separately on Schedule B, which is filed with the individual return.

Corporation tax returns are due on the fifteenth day of the third month following the close of the firm's taxable year. Individual and partnership returns are due on the fifteenth day of the fourth month. Never assume due dates with the IRS! Always coordinate the requirements with your accountant.

Self-Employment Tax

Self-employment tax represents social security payments for self-employed individuals. Independent businesspeople pay the highest social security rate of all (since they must make both the employer's and the employee's contribution), and the maximum increases every year. Self-employment tax is imposed on the taxable income (net profit) of your business. It is apart from and in addition to your federal income tax liability.

Sole proprietors and partners are liable for self-employment tax. Corporate stockholders are not. Self-employment tax is filed with your regular federal income tax return, using Schedule SE.

Estimated Income Tax

If your federal tax liability for a current year (income plus self-employment combined) is estimated to be $500 or greater, you may be required to pay your tax in quarterly installments to the IRS. Like taxes withheld from employee's paychecks, the government wants its share in advance.

Quarterly payments are due on April 15, June 15, September 15, and January 15. You do not have to pay the fourth estimate as long as you file your return by January 31, and pay the balance due.

How do you estimate your taxes? You have two options. First, you can base your estimate on your last tax year's income, divide it by four, and send that amount to the IRS every quarter. Second, you can estimate your taxes on the basis of your current income in this tax year. Each quarter, you figure your taxable income and send the IRS the correct tax. Be careful of this method, because the IRS can levy an interest penalty if you underestimate your income by more than 10 percent. Also, if you pay three low quarterly payments and you have a profitable year, beware of the tax-bite on April 15! You may have to make a whopper payment!

If you are a sole proprietor or partner, you are liable for estimated tax. Payments are submitted on a four-part form, 1040-ES.

Payroll Taxes

If your new firm has any employees, you will have certain obligations to the IRS for payment of payroll taxes and withholding of income taxes related to your employees' salaries in a given tax year. Similarly, you will probably have a tax-withholding obligation to your state and maybe your local jurisdiction. Discuss your obligations with your accountant!

Although the IRS does not prescribe any particular form in which your payroll records must be kept, you should incorporate the following as good practice:

1. Each employee's name, address, and social security number.

2. The amount and period of each wage payment.

3. The amount of wages subject to withholding included on each wage payment.

4. The amount of tax withheld and date collected.

5. Your employer identification number. (If you do not have one, call the IRS and obtain Form SS-4 to file for one.)

6. Duplicate copies of all returns filed.

7. Dates and amounts of deposits made with the IRS.

8. Your employees' withholding exemption certificates (Form W-4).

There are three types of federal payroll taxes that you must withhold:

Income taxes

Social security taxes (FICA)

Federal Unemployment taxes (FUTA)

Income Taxes.   Income taxes are withheld on all wages paid to an employee above a determined minimum. The minimum is governed by the number of withholding allowances claimed by the employee.

Income tax deposits are made to the IRS on Form 501 through your bank. Depending on the amount, the taxes may be collected quarterly, monthly, or biweekly. The requirements for due dates are complex and should be coordinated with your accountant.

Social Security Taxes (FICA).   Social security taxes apply to a portion of wages paid to an employee during a particular tax year. Recently, the portion has been raised each year, so you should coordinate the current requirements with your accountant. The amount withheld from the employee's wage is matched by the company as the total tax.

Federal unemployment Taxes (FUTA).   During the tax year, employers are required to pay FUTA taxes on each employee's first $4200 of wages paid. You may receive a credit against your federal unemployment taxes for a certain percentage of the state unemployment taxes you pay. FUTA taxes are explained in depth on IRS Form 940.

State Taxes

Many states collect income taxes and have procedures and rules similar to federal regulations.

State income taxes, like federal income taxes, are based on your net income or net profit. Most states simply compute state tax as a percentage of the income shown on your federal return. Generally, you are allowed the same deductions and expenses that the feds allow. It is important to coordinate your state tax liability, strategy, and form processing with your accountant.

The IRS and You

The previous paragraphs should help you understand why a general knowledge of the IRS and its internal workings will benefit you in your dealings with the government. More than likely, like the majority of individuals and businesses filing returns, you will never get audited. The fact of the matter is that the IRS audits less than 2 percent of all tax returns filed!

All federal returns are automatically checked by computer for errors. If one is found, it does not increase your chances of an audit. What is important to remember is that returns that are audited are those that are obviously out of line with the IRS' idea of the "norm." When returns are recorded on computer tape for archiving at the regional IRS service centers and then sent to the national computer center in Martinsburg, West Virginia, they are inspected and compared with what is known as the DIF (discriminate input function) formula. This DIF is a computer program of the average American's financial profile. If your return is within the DIF formula, you are deemed an honest taxpayer, and you will probably never hear from the IRS about your return. If your return is outside the DIF, IRS agents will review it, and if they think the return is a potential money-maker for the government, they will audit you.

You can generally expect the IRS to look at the following items on your return:

Unusual or unreasonable business expenses

Large deductions for entertainment

An unreasonable profit, comparing total expenses with total income

Inconsistency from one year to the next

Discuss these items with your accountant, and get his or her opinion and recommendations on them as well as on other matters. Chart 11 lists typical business expenses that are allowable as IRS deductions.

Any significant changes in your return from year to year will invite an IRS review—and possible audit. If you ever had the pleasure of an IRS audit, or experience one in the near future, your chances of being audited again are increased. The IRS, unlike lightning, does strike the same person twice or even more!

Declaring a business loss on your tax return does not automatically cause an audit. A loss, however, will more likely be examined by the IRS. It is common for companies with large start-up costs and slow business to report a loss in their first year. However, after the first year, if a business shows continued losses, and does not show a profit for at least three out of five consecutive years, the IRS has the power to determine that the business is a "hobby" and to disallow any losses! IRS agents will allow ongoing losses if they are convinced during an audit that the taxpayer is operating a real business and trying to make a profit.

Failure to File a Return

In today's world of computers, the IRS isn't infallible, and it isn't big brother looking over your shoulder. The IRS doesn't know everything! Why, then, bother to file a return, especially for incidental income?

In the design business, there is a reasonable chance that you have conducted some moonlight work for smaller projects during your tenure at your current or former employer. If you didn't (or do not) report this income to the IRS, you failed to file a comprehensive, accurate return. You realized financial gain, and Uncle Sam didn't share in it!

Some clients may want to pay for your services in cash, thus eliminating any paper trail of money spent and avoiding tax liabilities. Be careful! Only you can make the decision on whether to accept this form of compensation. It is tempting to say yes, and not record or report the income! This is being intentionally dishonest, and may lead to further problems. If you elect to accept cash for payment of services, treat it similar to tips received by waiters and waitresses. Report the income on Form 1099, as a supplement to your W-2 form from your employer.

What generally happens is that a moonlighter will work for years, and receive $5000, $10,000, or $20,000 over time. If you do not report the income and the IRS audits you and finds out, look out! You will be subject to pay all back taxes plus penalties and interest accrued! A no-win situation. Be careful, and think twice before conducting work without paying taxes. Finally, make sure you save all your tax returns. Inevitably, whenever you have the future need for capital, your potential banker will request several years of returns for review.

CHART 11
Typical Business Expenses Allowable As IRS Deductions

Accounting fees
Accounting records format
Advertising
Auditing fees
Automobile expenses

Bad debt expenses
Bank service charges
Bookkeeping services
Books with useful life of one year or less
Business associations
Business cards
Business gifts
Business licenses

Charitable contributions
Cleaning expenses
Coffee service
Collection expenses
Consultant fees
Conventions
Credit card fees

Depreciation
Dues: business associations/ professional societies

Education expenses
Electricity
Employer's taxes

Entertainment
Equipment

Insurance
Interest on business debt

Janitorial services

Legal expenses
License fees

Magazines
Minor repairs
Moving expenses

Office furnishings
Office in the home
Office supplies

Passport fees (for business trip)
Payroll and withheld payroll taxes
Periodicals
Postage
Property taxes

Rent

Safe deposit boxes
Salaries
Security system monitoring services
State income tax

(Continued)

Stationery

Supplies

Telephone

This book!

Travel away from the office on business

Utilities

Summary

The basic rules to remember with the IRS are the following:

1. Know the filing dates for your business's taxable year.
2. Document every expenditure and income source as if you expected an audit notice from the IRS tomorrow.
3. Don't miss a payment, because if you do, it takes forever to get out of the IRS computer.
4. The IRS is *always* right, most of the time!

Don't be fearful of the Internal Revenue Service. Instead, use it as a motivating factor, a prod to your business conscience, to keep accurate and documented records.

6
Banking Considerations

"I'll never forget the first time I went to the large bank on the corner to open my company's commercial checking and savings account. I had $2000, my life savings, and the bank politely told me to come back in a few years when the business was larger and successful. I have never forgotten that moment. It has driven me throughout the years to the point that our firm now does over $250,000 per year in business with that bank, designing its branches and offices, but we do not have our corporate accounts there. I wonder why?"

"I'll never forget the couple of days before I officially opened my new company's doors. I went to the "big" bank on the corner and asked for the necessary forms to open a new commercial checking and savings account. When I told the banker that I had $200 to put in both accounts, I was advised to "come back when I had more money"! Then, I went down the street to the other "big" banks, and I couldn't believe that they said the same thing. Here I was, experiencing one of the most incredible highs of my life, starting my own firm, and boy did those bankers blow my ego!

I then got some advice from a business friend to talk to his banker, who was with a smaller bank and related well with start-up businesses. When I met with this "smaller banker," I was very careful not to take out my frustrations on him, but also I was concerned about "going down in flames" again! I decided to level with him, and after 10 minutes my new firm had two bank accounts confirmed on a handshake with my new banker. I will never forget him, because he listened to me, understood my concerns, and believed in me."

Your relationship with your bank is your financial lifeline. The process of selecting a bank (and a banker) is a critical one, and you should discuss your firm and business plan with at least six institutions before you select one.

Ask your accountant and lawyer which bank and bankers they recommend. These are probably the most effective introductions. If a banker has an ongoing relationship with a professional who is advising you as a client, a less impersonal relationship will exist, and there is a better chance that more careful decisions will be made about your needs. Rely on your network of contacts.

Banking Services

When you are selecting a bank for your new firm, consider the services offered. Sure, on the surface, all banks appear to be full service. What does full mean? Compare the services of each candidate bank. You may be surprised at what you find. Each bank may treat a particular service differently.

Also, investigate the fees associated with banking services. Does the bank charge a fee for check writing? Deposits? (Imagine, some banks charge *you* to deposit money in their bank!) Monthly savings accounts? Are there any limitations on how many checks you can write per month on a particular account? The following are standard services offered by most banks for start-up businesses:

Commercial checking accounts

Small business checking accounts

Business savings accounts

Commercial money market accounts

Payroll accounts

Cash management services

Short-term loans

Long-term loans

Lines of credit

Letters of credit

Automatic teller machine (ATM) usage

Take your time when evaluating candidate banks and their services. Make sure the bank's service offerings meet or exceed your new firm's banking requirements. There is nothing worse than having a bank that doesn't understand your business, that can't or will not help you grow. Further, it is frustrating if your bank is too big and treats you and your firm as "small potatoes."

Before you meet with any bankers, it is important to understand where bankers come from. They are trained to be skeptical and always require two sources of repayment on loans. The primary sources of repayment are cash flow for short-term loans and earnings for long-term loans. All deals with bankers are backed up with some form of collateral such as accounts receivables or assets. Then, if something goes wrong with the original payment plan, the banker always has at least one fall-back position.

When you are starting your firm, the first rule in selecting a financial institution is, Pick a banker, not a bank. As we discussed in the selection process for lawyers and accountants, select a banker who is genuinely interested in your new firm and understands architecture and the practice of it.

The second rule is as follows: Every loan officer in a bank is a vice president; therefore, forget big titles and pick a young, aggressive loan officer and gain his or her confidence. How do you gain the confidence of the loan officer? The first rule of "selling the banker" is to exhibit confidence in yourself as well as your new company. Bankers thrive on track records, so when you are starting out with no record, you may feel it is an impossible feat to sell the bank. This is where your self-confidence and communication skills come in. Both will play an integral part in the future success of your firm. Before you meet and interview potential banks and loan officers, you must do your homework. When you visit each bank, have the following information with you:

Preliminary business plan

Your current résumé

Projected operating budget

Leave copies of these with all your potential lenders, even if you are not asking for a loan and are just inquiring about opening a commercial checking and savings account. You will be perceived as being extremely organized and confident, and thus a lesser risk to the bank. That is what banking is all about—a game of risk. Banks sell money and services that deal in money.

The third rule to follow when you visit the banks is that you are doing banks a favor by bringing your new enterprise to them. Banks may control all the money, but without you and your new firm, they can't make any money on their money!

The fourth rule is to make your potential banker your silent partner. Sell your banker on the fact that your new firm is viable and potentially profitable, and that you may not need loan capital at this stage, but you do need the bank's expertise in helping you operate and grow. You will be surprised how many banks, especially the big ones, do not want to help small businesses (not to mention new design service businesses) start out! They feel that they will lose money because the new ventures will need only checking accounts and will maintain minimal savings accounts. Also, do not be surprised if a bank extends an offer to your new company contingent on gaining *all* your personal banking requirements.

Once you make a decision and select your new banker and bank, you'll soon learn that they will expect you to personally countersign for any loans that you ask for. Don't let this throw you. How many people you know say that they would never sign any such thing? They would sign only "unsecured" loans. Well, the fact of the matter is that when the bank asks you to personally guarantee a loan request, it's the only way it has to certify your numbers and your confidence in what you are doing. Asking for a loan is a double-edged sword. Don't take the responsibility lightly. It's easy for any new firm to be overly optimistic. Before you sign that note, read all the fine print, and take a good hard look at all the figures. Your signature is more than an autograph!

Bank policies change from time to time, and a design firm can be looked upon as an increasing risk. If the real estate market is in a slump, for example, your bank could make a policy decision to be very cautious about existing or pending loans related to real estate deals. Therefore, since you as a designer deal in the real estate industry, your banking relationship could be adversely affected. If you think the bank is concerned, prepare a realistic assessment and business plan of how you intend to deal with the situation.

What Do Bankers Know About the Design Business?

Most new design firms start when the overall economy is weak or in a stage of recovery, or when the economy is overwhelmingly strong. Bankers have little information available to them regarding the basic characteristic of design firms and their financing needs. Lenders usually pay specific attention to the following characteristics of a firm:

Firm reputation

Variety of client base

Cash flow patterns

Insurance coverage

Most design firms are small and privately held. Of the more than 100,000 design firms in the United States, fewer then 100 are publicly held. The reason is that design firms are labor-intensive and usually operate with a staff of fewer than 50 employees to maintain control. Also, managers of design firms typically prefer more professional autonomy than their counterparts in larger firms. Small design firms need less financing in the initial stages of operation because they are primarily levering up managerial talent.

The capital structure of design firms varies with the type of organization. Sole proprietorships and partnerships rely extensively on the owner's capital. Historically, start-up firm owners and partners have been reluctant to relinquish the autonomy that comes with limited credit restrictions imposed by banks; therefore, many new firms are undercapitalized. The design profession in general, being labor-intensive, allows for small and thinly capitalized operations. Bankers pay special attention to the owner's reputations and background of experience.

Start-up design firms usually have two strikes against them in applying for loans with banks. First, they do not provide a standardized product or service. Second, the owner is usually considered a designer—that is, someone who is technically competent but has no formal financial or management training.

Bankers realize that many new design firms begin as spin-off companies. The founder is a classic entrepreneur, who is not always motivated by profits but whose mission in life is to implement his or her ideas in a way that could not be done in the old firm. Client loyalty—the focus of the marketing plan—relies heavily on the reputation of the firm as a whole, and in many cases on the individuals within the firm. Many a new firm's portfolio is comprised of contracts with clients from the owner's prior place of employment.

The geographic locale of a design practice also has an impact on how bankers view the new business. It has been estimated that the western and southern regions of the United States will experience the greatest population growth in the 1990s. In reviewing a credit application, many a banker analyzes the relationship between the range of services the design firm expects to provide and the local demand environment evidenced by demographic trends.

Insurance coverage also plays a major role in a banker's review of a new firm. Many new firms intentionally plan to "go bare"—that is not carry professional liability insurance. Many banks will view this as poor risk management, and will allow the firm to have checking and savings accounts but will not provide any credit line because of the potential liability exposure. Commercial banks may require new firms with partners to carry keyperson insurance, designed to cover lost billings if a key individual leaves the firm or dies. In the case of death, the insurance also covers the stock liquidation payments.

Because reputation and referral commissions are critical to a design firm, loan officers will check the reputation of your firm and its individual registered professionals. They will contact local licensing boards to verify licensure and the existence of any record of reprimands. They will check with suppliers and consultants that they have a banking relationship with as to your firm's credibility and creditworthiness.

Finally, bankers will evaluate the mix of business or clients that you have. If you have one large client, or only one client, don't expect a loan. The bank will ask the logical question: "What if your client goes bankrupt? How will you repay your loan if you lose all your business?"

What Characteristics Do Bankers Look For in a New Design Firm?

As stated in the preceding section, start-up firms usually have a few "strikes" against them with bankers when it comes to creditworthiness. New design firm owners typically come to a bank with no track record or history in the field as business owners.

Here are a few things that bankers evaluate when they are approached for credit:

1. Bankers prefer that a new owner operate the particular firm for at least a year prior to approaching the bank. During this time, the new firm will have developed a clientele and referral network. Bankers recommend that during this first year, the new firm save money to help support itself. Banks prefer not to provide funds to pay the salaries of owners.

2. Bankers like to see a new firm rely on an accountant and a lawyer for assistance in developing business projections and business plans. Bankers are more comfortable when you bring these professional advisors with you to talk to them.

3. Bankers look for a "sound" second source of repayment of the credit amount should the firm fail. This second source could be inside or outside the company (i.e., a strong co-borrower). The source can be waived in the future when the company grows stronger.

4. The company and owner should be of upstanding character—honorable and trustworthy. Bankers want to know how you will react when times get tough.

5. The customer must have the capacity to repay the loan. If your company is not profitable or has poor cash flow, chances are the bank will not extend credit. Remember, banks are in the business of lending money, and getting paid back!

6. The borrower should be adequately capitalized. This can provide the necessary cushion to help protect the bank if the firm fails or if business and economic conditions change. Banks look at savings accounts, stock portfolios, cash value of insurance policies, and so on.

7. Bankers like collateral. Having a tangible asset backing up each loan means that if anything goes wrong with the loan, the bank is covered.

Bankers review the above items as tried-and-true rules of good loan making. They are the core of sound commercial banking.

You will learn several things quickly if you deal with bankers:

Bankers will not be complacent in reviewing your account.

They will not be careless. There will be many "eyes" in the bank to review your account.

Bankers love to communicate and watch over your shoulder. They will be clear and concise with their information to you.

They will evaluate the competition of other banks, but not get carried away by it, because there will always be other businesses that need cash and credit.

Now that you have some understanding of bankers and what they look for in a new business, its accounts and potential credit, how do you apply for a loan?

Applying for a Loan

Many designers have a difficult time asking for money, whether it is from clients or from their banker. Getting the loan you request is a matter of selling yourself, and the better prepared you are, the more likely you are to be successful. Remember, you cannot assume that bankers will know everything about your firm, and it is your job to educate them. You begin this educational process by submitting a loan proposal containing the following items:

1. Loan request
    Purpose of the loan
    Amount required
    Term desired
    Source of repayment
    Collateral available

2. History and nature of the firm
    Brief two paragraphs

3. Updated business plan

4. Financial budgets (projected)

5. Financial information
    Balance sheet/income statement
    Personal financial statement

If you present this information in an organized fashion, you will be amazed at the favorable and enthusiastic response you will get from your banker! Why? Because only the top 1 percent of the bank's customers ever do such a thing. Your banker will be quite impressed. You will give the impression that you really know what you are doing and you will get what you ask for. Treat this exercise like a presentation of a conceptual design to a client: It is an exciting time for the project; you are proud of the product and will do everything in your power to convince the client to approve the design. Bring this same excitement to the banker's table, convincing the bank that it is helping not only your company but itself, because the loan will make your firm more profitable and thus develop the need for further growth and an expanded banking relationship.

Summary

Your banker will evaluate your loan request according to five Cs:

1. *Character.* Who are you? If you are not someone to be trusted, then the bank won't deal with you. This criterion is by far the most important.

2. *Capacity.* What is your financial strength and track record?

3. *Capital.* How much of your own money do you have invested?

4. *Collateral.* What is available to support the primary source of repayment?

5. *Conditions.* What is the economy doing and how will it affect your firm?

Finally, here are some dos and don'ts that will strengthen your banking relationship:

Do

Make regular appointments and allocate enough time.

Shoot straight; be honest.

Do your homework.

Ask questions if you do not understand anything.

Prepare a definitive plan.

Be flexible.

Don't

Be impatient.

Make promises that you can't keep.

Ask "how much" you can borrow.

Spend the money before you ask for it.

Ever surprise your banker.

7
Marketing Considerations

"If I am going to be working 16 hours a day, and I have enough work to keep myself busy, when do I market for the next job? How can I do two things at once: draw at my desk and market? What is marketing anyway? How can I promote myself if I am stuck at the office, or on a job site, or traveling all day? Where is the next project coming from?"

How Are You Going to Market Your New Firm?

Besides working on your first commission and writing a few checks to pay your start-up bills, somewhere along the line you must spend time focusing on what you want to do and how you plan to do it.

Since designers are deadline oriented and predominately procrastinators, they rarely take the time to plan and be proactive in marketing. Instead, they practice daily crisis management, putting out one fire after another. Who has time to think, let alone plan? The fact of the matter is that if you force yourself to take the time in the evening or on the weekend—time away from the prime 40-hour week—to plan your new firm's direction, and step back every now and then to analyze your charted course, you will be very successful in doing work that you like to do. As a designer, you are paid to think, not react!

Now that you have your new headquarters, and you are armed to the teeth with your weaponry for business, how are you going to market all this? When you worked at the old firm, all you did was design, or do production drawings or administration. How do you learn to market? How will you market your services? Do you know the difference between selling and marketing?

What Is Marketing?

Marketing is an essential process for success in the design business. It is a process that involves a wide spectrum of activities, both direct and indirect, with the ultimate goal of convincing clients that you and your firm are sensitive to their needs and can be trusted to solve their design problems.

There are only two kinds of marketing: direct and indirect.

You engage in *direct marketing* when you become aware of a particular project, write the requisite letter, make the necessary phone call, go and visit the potential client, and hope for an interview and selection.

You are engage in *indirect marketing* in literally everything else you do from the moment you arise in the morning until you retire in the evening. You market indirectly by going to church, shopping for food, attending a little league baseball game, or making a deposit at the bank. The importance of indirect marketing is that you never know whom you will meet. Anyone could be a potential client or referral. Someone could just pop up on a building committee. You market indirectly every waking hour of the day. This also holds for any partner(s) you may have. In fact, any employee that you engage in the future will be an ambassador of the firm.

Studies have shown that indirect marketing is more important than direct marketing to a design firm because most of its commissions come through a contact referral network or through the recommendations of satisfied clients.

Many designers fail in business because of poor marketing. Some do not appreciate the necessity of marketing; others do not know how to market. Some do not like to market and still others do not want to market. If you fit into one or more of these categories, make sure you find a partner who doesn't. Or just learn to tolerate marketing and do it, because if you don't, failure is not far around the corner.

Should You Consider Retaining a Marketing Consultant?

Many designers who do not enjoy marketing, or who feel they do not have good marketing skills, think that the answer is to hire a full-time marketing person to fill the void. Many expect a marketing expert to provide new projects within a short period of time. The fact of the matter is that potential clients must be cultivated. Marketing seeds take many months, if not a year, to germinate once they are planted. Marketing consultants are indirect, long-term salespeople for a firm, not short-term solutions for business development.

Marketing consultants can help you focus on strengthening your marketing skills. They can write press releases and distribute them to newspapers and magazines. They can prepare brochures or edit newsletters for the firm. And they can help you develop a contact network for future prospects. Most important, they can help you forge the correct image for your new firm and show you how to communicate it to the outside world.

Marketing consultants cost money. For a start-up firm, a full-service consultant may be unaffordable. However, consider retaining one on an hourly basis to help you focus on your immediate, midrange, and long-term marketing goals. Later on in this section, you will learn how to develop a preliminary marketing plan. Review your initial draft with a marketing consultant, for an outsider's opinion.

As your company grows and changes, your needs for a marketing consultant will evolve. If you elect to retain the services of one, schedule quarterly meetings to review your firm's progress and monitor and record your marketing goals.

Image

A major issue that you must address—whether alone, with your partner(s), or with a marketing consultant—is what image you want your new firm to have. Image is directly related to the vision that you have for the firm and its future. Whatever vision you have, the image must be consistent, or you will not get on track and achieve the results you need for success. Your thoughts on "image" affect every decision that you make in the day-to-day operation of your firm.

Some designers set too high an image, one that they cannot afford to obtain or maintain. A designer with aspirations to create residential architecture certainly does not need the same image as a health-care designer who wants to design large hospital projects. Similarly, if you work alone, you do not need the image of a 500-person firm!

Image is projected in your company's name and letterhead, in your office, even in the clothes you wear! Like it or not, your behavior, your appearance, and the image of your firm are all impressions that the world will judge you on as you make the journey toward success in business and in life.

One of the challenges you will face at the outset is that if your markets are varied, you will need to be flexible and project different images. For many designers who have only one market, this is not a problem. However, if an opportunity occurs outside your niche, you must make a careful decision. Do you belong in that particular market? Can you be successful in it? If you get involved in it, where might it lead you? How does it compare with your current market(s)? Will it mix in well? Are you qualified to do a project in the new market, or will you consider hiring another to produce the project? Sounds complicated, doesn't it?

Most new firm owners are entrepreneurs who do not like to say no to opportunities. They see a particular project as income, and say yes without considering the big picture. If you are an owner who can't say no to opportunities, get ready for a complex, potentially schizophrenic marketing experience. Your firm may have a variety of images, and you'll need to dress for success in each different arena.

Clearly, you would consider wearing different clothing to an interview with a large corporate client than to one with a residential customer who seeks a home addition. Residential customers may be overwhelmed by a "corporate image" suit and may feel that they cannot afford your services or are too small for your firm. Of course, your company may not have the opportunity to work in both arenas. However, when opportunity knocks, you must seize it!

The fact of the matter is that your image will change throughout the life of the firm. So, start out striving for a strong, realistic, obtainable image. The reality is, if you are a sole proprietor and attempt to market yourself as a large firm, that particular, sophisticated client type will probably not retain your services because you lack depth. If you were trained in a large firm with a speciality, say, in health care, focus on the smaller health care projects within hospitals, outpatient clinics, and physician's offices. Your former employer's clients are contacts, and they may be willing to commission you to do smaller projects as a way of limiting their risk. At the same time, they will obtain good value, because the large firm may be more expensive and not put its "first string" designers on the small project.

Most important, make sure your firm's image is you, and what you are all about. Potential clients can see through a false image, or an image that you are uncomfortable with. For example, if a potential project involves designing a church, and you have never worked on one—or taken the time to talk to designers who have, or researched the topic—you will probably not project authority, confidence, expertise, and competence. The odds for your selection will be thin.

When you develop the right image—whether alone, with your partner(s), or with a marketing consultant—get comfortable with it, work with it, refine it. You will find success much quicker.

Selecting a Name

Selecting your new firm's name is an important decision from an image, vision, *and* legal perspective. It is essential to be aware of the implications of selecting your name and to make it work from the outset. As a design professional, you sell yourself and your ideas. Your firm's name should promote you. The image that you create for your firm begins with its name, how it looks written, how it works graphically with a logo, and how it sounds over the telephone. Choose a name that will serve you well for an indefinite period of time.

For many designers, their dream or vision has been "hanging a shingle" with their name on it. They want to let their creativity and imagination take charge. It is that simple! But before you do that, consider that a business name should be selected with care as well:

1. Choose a name that is both pleasant and easy to pronounce.

2. Choose a name that describes what you do. Compare:
   Franklin & Associates vs.
   Franklin & Associates, Architects

3. Do not select a name that will be limiting, unless you understand and accept the limitations. Compare:
   Kolscher Bridge Engineers vs. Kolscher Engineering Group
   Lavin Residential Interiors vs. Lavin Interiors Limited

Your firm's name will have an emotional impact on all who hear and read it. For example, if you decide to incorporate your name, George Apple, into George Apple AIA, Architect, most who encounter the name will assume that you are a sole proprietor with few or no employees. For many designers, this is what they are comfortable with, and what they desire.

If you want to project a larger, more established, or different image to the world, consider one of the following:

The Office of George Apple AIA, Architect

Apple + Company, Architects

George Macintosh Apple and Associates, Architects

Apple Architects, Inc.

Apple Architecture, Inc.

Apple + Associates, Architects

GMA Architects

What's in a name? Be careful of fictitious names or names that need an explanation to every client. Some clients feel that if you use a fictitious name, you are hiding behind it. To most, the name doesn't matter, because they have contacted *you* and want *you and your firm* to design the project. You will be amazed at the reception that you will get from potential clients just in the use of a name.

Remember, every time you change your company's name, you must change letterhead, business cards, telephone listings, signs, title blocks, office forms—the list goes on and on, and so do the associated costs! Apple & Associates will allow the inclusion of many professionals, associates, and partners for a greater period of time than will George Apple, Architect. The term "& Associates" projects an awareness of others—and their relative importance in the company—to the world as well as to employees!

Finally, whatever name you choose, especially if you incorporate, check with the secretary of state in your area to make sure that you do not infringe on another company's name.

Service Offerings

When you start your own firm, you need to organize your thoughts on what services you will be providing. This is not only for your benefit, but also for that of your clientele! I know it sounds so fundamental, but it is extremely valuable to document what services your firm can provide. Defining them will give you a better understanding of those service offerings that you *won't* be producing, and will have to retain from consultants.

Your service offerings aren't just limited to the name of your profession! Much of the client public doesn't understand precisely what architecture, engineering, or interior design is. If you told 100 people that you were an interior designer, you would probably get 100 different reactions.

If you intend to provide services for different markets, you may want to have different lists of services for each market. You may feel qualified to perform master planning services for religious facilities, but not for hospitals, for example. Take the time to evaluate what your strengths are for each market that you can provide services for, and make a list for your benefit as well as for your potential clients! Chart 12 summarizes typical service offerings for a design firm.

Niche Markets

What are niche markets? When designers specialize by project type, some develop very profitable specialties, or niches. All designers have strengths and weaknesses. As a new firm owner, you need to capitalize on your strengths. If your background is in residential design, you need to hone your strengths and develop a niche in the residential market in your area.

To analyze your strengths or competencies, evaluate yourself in the following categories:

Design

Service

Technical competency

Delivery capability

Project cost knowledge

Schedule requirements

Fees

If you feel that you master all of the above in a particular market segment, then establish that segment as a niche—and market, market, market! Develop a vision and image for that niche. Develop a marketing plan that

CHART 12
Typical Design Service Offerings

Facilities Management

Inventory existing space allocations

Field survey existing space and equipment

CADD documentation of existing facilities

Master plan development

Interior Design

Programming

Space planning

Interior finish selection

Furniture specification

Existing furniture inventory

Architecture

Feasibility studies

Design

Historic preservation

Construction documents

Bid/negotiation phase services

Construction administration

In-house cost estimating

Expert testimony

Postoccupancy services

Engineering

Feasibility studies

Design

Construction documents

Bid/negotiation phase services

Construction administration

In-house cost estimating

Value engineering

Forensic engineering

Energy consulting

CADD Systems

Autocad version 10

Intergraph microstation PC 3.3

Planning

Programming

Master planning development

Feasibility studies

(Continued)

addresses the niche. Market your niche indirectly; and sell your background and service capabilities to direct-market opportunities.

Once you have the direct-market lead and offer your service capabilities, the potential client, feeling comfortable with your background and firm, will probably ask for a proposal for professional services. One-third of the battle is won by getting in the door; the next third is to convince the client in writing that you can solve the particular problems involved. (The final third, of course, is getting the job done!)

Find a niche in a market that needs the services of a firm like yours. It may not be easy, but think about it. Observe and talk to people; network with others to learn what is going on in your community and the local business arena. Get the word out that your firm is available to help others solve their problems. Keep track of all your leads as if they were gold. Remember, if someone refers you to a possible project, his or her neck is on the line as well as yours! Be aggressive and proactive in marketing the services of your firm.

Writing a Proposal That Sells

The formal way to sell your capabilities and services is through a written proposal. Proposal writing is an art. There are as many opinions on writing proposals as there are ways to do so. Remember, always personalize your proposals. Customize each one. Tell clients what you perceive to be their need, and how you plan to solve their problems and satisfy their needs. Be careful to express yourself clearly as to what services you feel each client needs, and those that you feel the client does not need. Proposals that are direct and to the point will be appreciated and will help sell your firm, because you will exhibit accountability and responsibility to your potential client. Your client will develop trust in your firm because your actions demonstrate care and concern.

Write your proposal following the format shown in Chart 13. It will give you and your client as close to a comprehensive document as possible. Before you begin, be sure to examine the sample proposal shown in Appendix A.

When you summarize your scope of services, use Chart 14 as a guide. It is a comprehensive checklist of design service tasks that are normally offered to clients. The list is generic, since there are no longer any "standard" or "normal" services on a design project.

Your firm's policy is that it cannot begin work without an executed proposal.

Enforce this rule on yourself and all your clients. At best, potential problem clients will recognize that you are business oriented and treat you accordingly. Also, some clients may warrant a formal contract. A signed proposal will allow you to begin work; you can then develop a formal contract to be executed before the design of the project is completed.

If there is one fundamental mistake that designers make more than others it is in proposal/contract preparation! Be concise, firm, and definitive. Most important, write the proposal and get it executed!

CHART 13
Typical Proposal Format

I. *Scope of Work*

Summarize what the client has told you, and what the client expects of you. Be explicit and complete. There are never enough words to describe a client's expectations. Then tell the client how you plan to organize your capabilities into a scope of work. List the phases to be detailed below.

II. *Phases*

Describe each phase, when and how it begins, what you will be doing, and what the product of the phase is. How many meetings will you have with the client? Define the time frame (schedule) and associated fee for each phase. Describe how the phase ends, and how it leads into the next phase

III. *Summary of Fees*

Summarize all fees by phase and total the "bottom line."

IV. *Exclusions*

Tell the client what you specifically have *not* included in your scope of work. Be precise, and do not worry about using too many items or words. This may be the most important section of your proposal, because the client may recognize certain items—not in your scope of work (or in your fee)—that he or she wants to include in the project.

V. *Additional Services*

Tell the client that anything not mentioned in the scope of work is excluded and considered an additional service. State that your firm will be delighted to take on additional services. You will quote the client a fee for each request based on your standard hourly rates. List your rates.

VI. *Reimbursable Expenses*

It is important to differentiate between services and expenses. Tell the client that you will charge for automobile mileage, printing, photography, long-distance telephone communications, and other expenses associated with the project.

(Continued)

VII. *Miscellaneous Provisions*

This section reinforces certain points that are discussed in the other six sections. Here is where you make your proposal complete. Stress important issues such as payment terms, terms of the proposal effectiveness, interest on late payments, down payments, and your right to withhold drawings if the client has not paid. Most important in your last paragraph describe how important the project is to you and how you look forward to working with the client.

VIII. *Acceptance*

Develop language that the client will acknowledge and sign to bind your services.

Selling

Selling is different from marketing. Selling is *part* of marketing.

Selling is promoting yourself and your talents to potential clients. Selling is convincing clients that you can help them solve their problems. You must sell the importance of human chemistry, reliability, service, design, accountability, and genuine care for the client. Selling is not sending out a form letter, or advertising in a magazine.

Once you have done your job of indirect marketing, you will have leads to begin your direct-marketing phase. The potential client has asked for a proposal from your firm—as well as from three other firms! How is the client going to make a decision?

Even before you develop your proposal, you need to ask the client a few questions to help you demonstrate that you are overwhelmingly interested in the project, and that you care for the client's needs. The answers that you receive will tell you a lot about the project, the client, and your chances of being commissioned to do the work! Tailor your proposal around the client's answers to the following questions— to separate your firm from the rest of the pack (the competition):

What do you have in mind for the project?

What are your needs on the project?

Is anyone against the project?

What is the funding source for the project?

If my firm is selected, with whom will it be under contract and accountable to?

CHART 14
Typical Design Service Tasks

Predesign Services

Project-related research

Predesign conferences

Development of fees and contracts

Reviewing owner data for project

Procuring existing drawings of site or building

Programming spatial requirements

Evaluating site requirements

Documentation of existing conditions

Photography
Field measurement
Drafting of existing conditions

Analysis of existing engineering capabilities

Structural
Mechanical/electrical/plumbing

Marketing studies

Feasibility studies

Preliminary project budgeting and scheduling

Presentations of any of the above

Site Analysis Services

Procuring necessary surface/subsurface site data

Procuring title information on property

Procuring new survey data

Site photography

Agency/jurisdiction review and approval process

Zoning process services

(Continued)

Community organization review and approval process

Environmental group review and approval process

Site analysis

Site development planning

Site utility studies

Environmental studies and delineation

Project budgeting and scheduling

Presentation of any of the above

Conceptual Design Services

Conceptual design sketches

Study models

Perspective sketches

Conceptual engineering design requirements

Agency/jurisdiction review

Project budgeting and scheduling

Presentation of any of the above

Owner approval process

Design Refinement (Development) Services

Refined plans of conceptual design

Refined elevations, sections, details of conceptual design

Engineering design refinement drawings

Outline specification of material selections

Study model

Refined perspective sketches

Agency/jurisdiction review

Estimate of probable construction costs

Project scheduling

Presentation of any of the above

Owner approval process

Construction Document/Permit Document Services

Development of documentation for construction and permit application

Engineering documentation for construction and permit application

Specifications for material selections

Final models

Professional renderings

Agency/jurisdiction review

Estimate of probable construction costs

Project scheduling

Presentation of any of the above

Owner approval process

Bid/Negotiation Phase Services

Compilation of bidding material

Identification and procurement of bidders

Prequalification of bidders

Prebid meetings

Coordination and answering questions during bid phase

Development of addenda for clarifications

Procuring bids

Attending bid opening

Evaluation of bids

Assisting owner in awarding contract

Participation in negotiations

Assisting owner in notifying all bidders of results

Assisting in developing contract agreement forms

(Continued)

Assisting owner in developing notice to proceed

Construction Phase Services

Office services

Review of submittals
Telephone coordination
Coordination of change order requests
Interpreting intent of documents
Preparing clarification drawings
Project schedule monitoring
Procurement of all releases of liens
Issuance of certificate of substantial completion
Record documentation/maintenance manuals
Issuance of final approval for payment to contractor

On-site services

Review of progress
Review of contractor's payment requests
Punch list documentation
Final walk-through

Special Services

Special studies

Renderings

Life-cycle cost analysis

Value architecture/engineering analysis

Professional cost estimating services

Environmental/energy analysis

Graphic design

Project marketing artwork development

Expert witness testimony

Special engineering consultant coordination services

Any service not listed above pertinent to design

Is a committee involved in the presentation process? Who are the members of the committee, and what do they do for a living?

Who makes the decision on awarding the contract?

Have you or your organization ever worked with a design professional before?

Whom?

Who are the other design professionals my firm is competing with?

What kind of fee structure do you have in mind?

What is your estimated budget for the project?

After the presentations and proposals are made, how long will it take to award the contract?

While you are direct-marketing for the potential project, you also need to ask your client about the criteria for selecting a design professional. The following list incorporates most of the criteria clients use in comparing designers:

Does the designer understand the project?

Does the designer understand my/our needs?

Does the designer have the experience/background to perform?

How long will it take the designer to perform the services?

How much will it cost?

Once you determine the criteria for selection, address them in your proposal! Identify the client's "hot buttons" in boldface or italics. Show the client that you care. You listened and took the time to effectively communicate how you will address the client's needs better than the competition! This is selling.

Clients will review your proposal as well as submissions from the competition and will develop certain perceptions about each competitor. Clients will probably compare your firm with competitors on the following points:

Is the firm large or small, and can its size meet our expectations for the project?

Is the firm local or out of town, and can its location meet our expectations?

Is the firm an expert or a novice in this project type?

Many clients select the designer who "wants to design our project the most"! Other clients base their selection primarily on price. Still others want "name" firms only and are simply shopping the project, asking your firm (and others) for a proposal to use as a negotiating tool with the "name" firm. Determine early in the direct-marketing stage what type of potential client you have.

After you have done your indirect and direct marketing, find out the type of potential client you have, and write a proposal. You may be asked to make a presentation or meet with the client to explain your proposal and answer questions.

When you meet face to face with your potential client, remember that selling with smooth words and hot phrases is one thing. Substance is another. When you deliver the presentation, do it with enthusiasm, confidence, authority, professionalism, and above all commitment to the project! Every client is different, and will react differently to certain selling techniques. *You must tailor each and every presentation to that particular client.*

Many designers have found out the hard way that lengthy slide shows of their work—a staple of the past—have become boring as a sales technique. Clients obviously want to know about you and your firm's experience; but their major concern is how you are going to help *them*! When you darken the lights and show slide after slide of your work, the presentation becomes a "one way street," with very little interaction and dialogue. If you must show slides, keep them to a minimum. Strategically place a few visuals in your presentation as "teasers" to entertain the client.

Your selling skills will improve with experience and over time. Be patient. You will make plenty of mistakes. Many a designer has spent enormous amounts of time in indirect and direct marketing only to "blow it" when it came to selling the job. The most important thing you can do in this case is to attempt to get debriefed by the client. Get the client's impression of the presentation, and learn from it. You never know when that client will give you a chance again in the future. The next time, you will be a little more savvy, experienced, and prepared. Selling takes practice, practice, and more practice!

Summary

Thus, when you market yourself and your firm, you must carefully calculate the image that you want to create. You and your marketing efforts must project authority, confidence, friendliness, accountability, responsibility, vision, and leadership.

Marketing is not selling. Selling is only a part of marketing! Selling is getting a client to agree to hire you and your firm. Marketing is a way of life.

Remember, your vision in indirect marketing, direct marketing, and selling is to get the client to say yes. Structure your selling strategy so that you are comfortable with your offering to the client. Effectively say what you will do, and then back it up by doing what you say. A solid, quality reputation is one of the major selling tools that a firm can have.

8
Legal Considerations

"Can I afford to retain a lawyer? Lawyers are so expensive! Maybe I can go to the library and read up on the legal issues and do it myself. Why do I need a lawyer? Why can't I just practice architecture, and not worry about legal issues? Why must I be so organized, or appear that way?"

"I'll call a lawyer when I really need one."

"Partnership agreements, buy-sell agreements, articles of incorporation—why is business so complicated? All I want to do is design! No one told me about all this legal jazz."

"I wonder if I should have an attorney review this contract."

Do I Need a Lawyer to Help Start My Firm?

There is a very simple answer to this question: yes.

Every business decision has legal implications, every decision! The fatality rate of small businesses is enormously high. The odds are about 10:1 that your firm will fail in the first three years of its existence! Therefore, it is extremely important that you establish a sound legal foundation for the new firm. However, as discussed in previous chapters, keep your organization simple. You do not have to hire legal corporate counsel that has a worldwide reputation.

Types of Legal Counsel

There are two types of lawyers that you will need to help you start your firm. (Some designers are fortunate to find a lawyer who can assume both roles.) First, you need a lawyer who understands small business, whose practice is centered around it. Such lawyers genuinely care about their small business clients; they have the same attitude toward the health of a fledgling firm as a physician has toward the health of a patient. This kind of legal counsel will help you decide what form of business to establish and will process the necessary paperwork with the local jurisdiction.

The second kind of lawyer you will need is one who understands contract law, especially construction law and professional design agreements. If you are an architect, the American Institute of Architects' *Handbook on Professional Practice* has just about all the contract forms you will ever need. Still, it is advisable to retain counsel to review any special contracts or hybrids that may be prepared by your clients.

Retaining the services of counsel to discuss the many legal pitfalls of starting a new firm is a form of self-protection. All of us have felt the temptation to save money on legal fees in the beginning by purchasing guidebooks and looking for "free" advice. This is the worst thing we could do; we are trained as *designers*, not lawyers.

Selecting a Lawyer

How well you select your lawyer will have a direct impact on your firm's success. You should meet with at least three candidates before you make your selection. How do you get the names of three lawyers or firms? One of the most reliable methods is to get personal recommendations from your banker, from friends or colleagues, or from your local AIA/CEC/ASID office. Make sure that you interview lawyers who understand designers and the practice of design in your state. Make sure that your attorney has the proper credentials or professional designation (LLB or JD). Remember, though, that credentials and certification ensure only that an attorney has the minimum standard of education. There are no guarantees that the individual will be a creative business adviser with the necessary experience to fit your needs.

Fees will vary by the size of the firm and the experience of the lawyer. Firms with low rates may be concerned with high volume and not give you the attention that your new enterprise requires. High hourly rates tend to be associated with more conservative, less aggressive firms that are reluctant to spend time with small business clients, since their priorities rest with larger corporations. The lawyers in the middle fee range are the ones you should look for. They are in demand, however, because they are aggressive and innovative. Also, they care about small business—which accounts for 80 percent of business in the United States. It is important to be very open and discuss the lawyer's hourly rates, and what you will be getting for them.

Finally, select a lawyer whom you are most comfortable with and, most important, whom you will trust.

Forms of Business

Now that you have selected an attorney and are ready to set up your new firm, you need to understand what forms of business exist and which form is right for you. There are four forms of business for a start-up firm to consider: sole proprietorship, partnership, corporation, and Subchapter S corporation.

Sole Proprietorship

A sole proprietorship is the simplest form of business. The company is you and you are the company. In many cases, the only legality of this form of business is filing the appropriate tax returns. You must pay a quarterly estimate of your income tax and social security (self-employment tax), and you must retain all records of the business's transactions.

The following are advantages of starting as a sole proprietor:

Ease of formation

Low cost of registration and legal expense

Lack of complexity

Simple decision-making process

Sole ownership of profits

Ease of termination or sale of the firm

Flexibility

The following are disadvantages:

Unlimited personal liability

Less financing capacity with lenders (banks)

Unstable duration of the business owing to owner's illness or death

Sole decision making

Taxation on profits at certain levels

Limited business deductions

Unlimited liability is no doubt the biggest disadvantage. Many sole proprietors transfer title of their personal assets to their spouses to protect themselves from business liabilities! Another major disadvantage is that banks doubt the stability of sole proprietorships, since their success rests on one key individual. Finally, unlike corporations, sole proprietors cannot take the costs of automobiles, health insurance, and charitable contributions as business deductions.

Partnership

A partnership is a written or oral agreement between two or more parties to carry on a business. In a partnership, each partner contributes capital, services, and assets to share in the business's profit or loss.

An important issue in a partnership is that each partner is subject to unlimited personal liability for the debts of the partnership. Also, each partner is liable for the negligence of another partner and of the partnership's employees! Therefore, before you enter into a partnership, there are two concerns you should address:

1. If I go into partnership with _____, is this a responsible, accountable person whom I am going to be liable for?

2. Can I get enough insurance to adequately insure and protect the partnership, as well as my personal assets and my partner's?

As you can see, a partnership is significantly more complex than a sole proprietorship, although most states do not require any formalities of documentation. If your partnership does not have a formal "partnership agreement," your state law will determine the terms. State laws in general are based on fundamental characteristics of the partnership as it has existed throughout time. Here are the most important of the legally presumed characteristics:

1. No one can enter into a partnership without the consent and approval of all partners.

2. All partners have an equal vote in the operations of the partnership.

3. A simple majority vote is required for ordinary business decisions, and a unanimous vote is required to change the fundamental characteristics of the partnership.

4. All partners share equally in the profits and losses of the partnership.

5. A partner can withdraw from the business at any time, causing the partnership to dissolve.

These are just a few basics. Each state will have different presumed characteristics. Therefore, since each partnership is different simply because individuals are different, it is *highly recommended* that you employ counsel to help you draft a formal partnership agreement that recognizes your special requirements for a new design firm.

The major considerations that go into a partnership agreement include:

Name of the partnership

Description of the business

Capital contributions made by each partner

Duration of the partnership

Nature and degree of each partner's contribution

Business expenses and how they will be handled

Separate debts

Signing of checks

Draws or salaries

Absence and disability

Death of a partner and rights of continuing partners

Sale of partnership interest

Additions and modifications to the partnership agreement

Noncompetition agreements in the event of a partner's departure

Method of distributing profits

Management responsibilities

Duties of partners

Prohibited acts

Dissolution of the partnership

Given the complexities and potential problems involved in a partnership, it is surprising that so many designers operate without partnership agreements! Because of the nature of a partnership, it is essential to have an agreement.

The benefits and disadvantages of a partnership are similar to those of a sole proprietorship. Partnerships can be easy to form and "require" minimal paperwork. The greatest disadvantage is the potential conflict among the partners. Personal disagreements over the firm's operation or design approaches will hurt the business.

Business relationships often lead to good friendships, but friendships rarely survive a business relationship.

Nowhere is this truer than in a partnership.

The advantages of forming a partnership are:

Ease of formation

Pride of ownership

Direct rewards of profit (since more people are involved)

Greater availability of capital

Combination of expertise and talent

Flexibility

Relative freedom from government control and special taxation

The disadvantages are:

Unlimited liability

Conflict over terms of partnership agreement

Unstable duration of agreement

Management difficulties

Difficulty in obtaining large sums of capital from lenders (banks)

Difficulty of disposing of partnership interest

Corporation

A corporation is a legal entity that can be established by one or more individuals or legal entities. Its existence is separate and distinct from the individuals or other legal entities. The most important difference between a corporation and a partnership is the fact that the owners of the corporation (shareholders or stockholders) are *not* personally liable for the corporation's debts. For a small professional design corporation, however, this limited liability may be an illusion, since lenders often require owners to personally co-sign for any credit or loans. In addition, designers are personally responsible for their own wrongful or negligent acts.

Many start-up owners are tempted to form a corporation immediately because it underscores their decision and lends prestige to their firm. The corporate form, however, can be complex and very expensive to create and dissolve. As a designer, you would do well to work as a sole proprietor for at least a year to make sure that you have your act together. Starting business as a sole proprietor costs very little, reducing your capital requirements and lowering your overhead. After a year of experience, you should then explore the option of incorporating with your accountant and attorney.

The following are advantages of forming a corporation:

Limited liability of shareholders

Flexibility for tax planning

Corporate management flexibility

Financing readily available

Continued existence of corporation beyond death of a shareholder

Ownership readily transferable

Expertise available from more than one individual

The following are disadvantages:

Extensive government regulation

Activities limited by charter and bylaws

Majority shareholders can manipulate minority shareholders in voting

Expenses of incorporation process

Incorporating is generally a fairly simple matter, but to do it right the first time and to minimize costs and time, you should retain the services of an attorney. Since a lawyer's time is money, you can save both by using this checklist of points to discuss with your attorney:

Corporate name

Corporate structure

Names of officers

Names of shareholders

Shareholder agreements

Buy-sell agreement

Planning for future shareholders

Capitalization

Board of directors

Registered agent of the corporation (usually the incorporating attorney)

Most jurisdictions require "articles of incorporation" to be filed and approved before the corporation can conduct business. The articles summarize all of the above items.

Subchapter S (Sub-S) Corporation

If you elect the corporate form of business, you may wish to consider the advantages of a Sub-S corporation in the United States. Simply stated, the purpose of the Sub-S is to permit a small business corporation to treat its net income as though it were a partnership. This helps overcome the double taxation feature of the corporation, in which both corporate income and shareholder dividends are taxed. In addition, the Sub-S allows shareholders to offset business losses against their income. If a corporation anticipates losses during its first year or more, the Sub-S format may be desirable to minimize tax liabilities.

Again, this issue should be discussed with your accountant and lawyer, since Sub-S forms of incorporation are not recognized in all states.

Summary

The legal considerations involved in starting a new design firm include selecting an attorney who understands the needs of your new business and working *with* him or her to choose the form of business ownership that is right for you.

9

Insurance
Considerations

"I hate insurance sellers. They are worse than used car people! I avoid dealing with them."

"Why do I need insurance? No one is going to sue me! I care too much about my clients and their projects."

"Whole life vs. term, whole life vs. term. I've talked to three insurance agents, and am I ever confused!"

"I can't afford health insurance, so I hope my spouse keeps his job so that we retain coverage at his company."

"I can't possibly afford liability insurance. I'll just have to go naked for a while, and keep my fingers crossed."

Do I Need Insurance
When I Start My Firm?

Every new business venture represents a gamble, because it is difficult to predict the future. Even with adequate financing, a well-mapped business plan, and a backlog of projects to work on, the chances for success hover around the 50:50 mark at best! Business opportunities present a speculative risk which is two directional: win or lose. As in gambling, you may lose sometimes and then you may win. Hopefully you will win more than you lose. Luck is a factor here of course. However, there exist in life some one-directional risks—fire, death, disability—whose outcome is always a loss. Such one-directional risks are called *pure risks*. Insurance exists primarily to protect individuals and companies against losses caused by pure risks that damage property, life, or limb.

Accidents happen, people sue, disasters strike unexpectedly. You can't live in fear, wondering if a truck will hit you when you cross the next street. However, the sign of a good businessperson is the willingness to protect a business. It is imperative that you not only accept the existence of pure risk, but also learn how to live with it, and manage it. Proper risk management means planning for potential problems and attempting to insure against them. You must spend some time familiarizing yourself with the numerous types of insurance available on the market, and how to obtain them. Here are a few suggestions on developing your plan to protect your new firm from pure risks:

1. Think in terms of a well-planned program that starts out in a simple, affordable way, one that can grow with the business. As the firm grows, and you age, so will the risks. Therefore, don't buy too much insurance. But how do you know what is too much?

2. Seek professional help at the outset. Designers are certainly not experts in risks and insurance. Again, as in choosing a lawyer, accountant, or banker, you need to find a professional broker who understands small businesses, especially design firms. Most important, you need an insurance broker who genuinely cares about you and the success of your firm.

3. List your risk priorities. Insurance protection against a catastrophe should be near the top of the list (property and casualty). Professional liability insurance is also a major priority.

4. Hold down excessive costs by talking frankly with your broker, looking at several options in coverage, premiums, and deductibles. It is wise to investigate the advantages of package policies.

5. Keep accurate records of what your policies cover, so that in the event of a claim, you will have a complete listing for the insurance company and thus will diminish your firm's downtime.

6. Modify your insurance policies to changing conditions in your firm. Every time you purchase an asset, make sure it is covered. As the company grows and becomes more valuable, make sure the insurance coverage grows with it.

Businesspeople and entrepreneurs are often reluctant even to discuss pure risk because it is a negative, pessimistic topic that they have no control over. How many people do you know with the attitude "I can't worry about things I can't control"? Also, many people dislike meeting with insurance agents—whom they rank just below used car sellers—because they do not understand the fine points of insurance and feel that they are always being taken advantage of.

The fact of the matter is that we can't constantly worry about disasters and things we can't control, but as businesspeople, as risk takers, we must implement plans to "hedge our bets."

Obtaining Insurance

Insurance companies market their services chiefly through agencies, brokers, and clubs and associations.

1. *Agencies.* Agencies are smaller individualized operations that place home, car, and other common types of insurance with *several* insurance companies with whom they are affiliated. Since they must meet quotas with the different carriers, they may try to sell you policies that do not totally suit your needs or are not totally competitive.

2. *Brokers.* Brokers claim to have complete independence from any insurance company and offer more flexibility then any agency. Brokers usually have no vested interest in placing insurance with any particular company, and will therefore attempt to get you the best premiums and coverage to meet your needs. Talk to at least three brokers. If they are using the same insurance base for the best coverage and premiums, then all should recommend the same companies for the different forms of coverage you are requesting.

3. *Clubs and associations.* Contact your local better business bureau, chamber of commerce, or AIA chapter about its group insurance rates.

Types of Insurance

The types of insurance you will need will vary with your risks. The following overview of insurance policies is provided to make you aware of what exists and the types of insurance that might be appropriate. If you already have coverage (life insurance, car insurance, etc.), meet with your present agents to discuss your plans for your new firm. If they have been trustworthy to date with your personal insurance needs, they should be able to help you with your simple, start-up business insurance needs. Remember, after you conduct your research, only *you* can make the final decision on which insurance to select and purchase.

General Liability. A general liability policy covers losses due to bodily injury or damage to the property of others; all emergency, medical, and surgical expenses incurred from accidents; expenses to cover investigations; and your defense, settlement, and trial costs. The policy covers negligence causing injury to clients, employees, and the general public. It is normally written up as a comprehensive liability policy.

Completed Operations Liability. This policy offers protection against a lawsuit by a client who used your services and as a result sustained bodily injury or property damage.

Professional Liability (Errors and Omissions Liability). This coverage protects you and other design professionals on your consulting team against litigation arising from losses incurred by your clients as a result of a design error or omission.

Automobile Liability. This coverage includes other people's property, other automobiles, persons in other vehicles, and persons in the insured automobile. If you are using your personal car for business purposes, exclusively or occasionally, it is important that you have your premium cover business use. Problems can arise if you have an accident, and it is discovered that your car was indeed used for business purposes.

Fire and Theft Liability. If you operate your firm out of your home, you probably have fire and theft insurance. If you start your firm in an office outside your home, it is important to get coverage.

Business Interruption Insurance. The indirect loss from fire or theft can be greater than that of the loss itself. If your office is destroyed, you can lose revenue. Certain expenses must still be met. Such a situation can place a severe strain on your cash flow and jeopardize the survival of your business. Business interruption insurance is designed to cover the period of time between the loss and the return to normal operating conditions.

Overhead Expense Insurance.   This insurance covers the costs of fixed business expenses or overhead during your absence as a result of illness or accident.

Personal Disability Insurance.   There is a remote chance that you could become disabled for a short or long period of time. This insurance pays a certain monthly amount if you are permanently disabled, or a portion of that amount if you are partially disabled.

Key Person Insurance.   Your death or that of your partner or associate could seriously affect the earning power of your firm. If the key person dies, your existing clients may lose confidence, leading to the loss of future commissions, erosion of competitive position, loss of revenue, and the added expense of finding and/or training a replacement. Proceeds of the key person policy, with the firm as beneficiary, are generally not subject to income taxes. However, premiums are not a deductible business expense.

Partners or Shareholders Insurance.   Insurance for partners or major shareholders in a corporation is normally part of a buy-sell agreement which allows surviving partners or shareholders to purchase the deceased's interest in the company. In the absence of a buy-sell agreement funded by life insurance, the death of a partner could cause the immediate dissolution of the partnership in law. In the case of a corporation, without a buy-sell agreement the deceased shareholder's interest is considered an asset and goes to a beneficiary outlined in the deceased's will (if a will exists) or to the state. Most states have certain quotas requiring that designers make up the majority of stockholders in a design corporation. This could prohibit an unlicensed spouse from commanding the firm. However, why take the chance and have to deal with the consequences later?

Business Loan Insurance.   In many cases, your bank will require you to have insurance coverage for the outstanding amount of your loan and will incorporate the premium payments into the loan payment. In the event of your untimely death, the outstanding balance of your loan will be paid off.

Term Life Insurance.   Term life insures a person for a specified time period and then terminates. The most common period is five years. If the insured dies within the time period, the face value of the policy is paid to the beneficiaries. Since term life insurance does not have a cash or loan value, it is significantly less expensive than whole life insurance.

Medical Insurance.   It is important to have sufficient medical coverage for your needs. Some designers continue the coverage provided by their former employer or, if they have a working spouse, obtain coverage on the spouse's employer's plan. Usually, health insurance is prohibitively expensive for an individual. One option is to contact your local or state AIA chapter to see if there is a group plan for designers in the region. Other trade associations may offer medical insurance to their members. Group rates are substantially less than individual rates because of the size of the group and its buying power. However, some groups require you to have four or more employees to join. Policies offered by insurance companies vary, but medical and dental plans are available for small groups. When in doubt, ask your colleagues how they insure their firms.

Workers' Compensation Insurance.   Workers' comp requirements vary from state to state. However, when you hire employees, you will be required by your state law to provide some coverage. Fortunately, designers are considered to be in a low-risk profession and therefore have lower than average rates.

Professional Liability Insurance

Many designers ask the question, "Why do I need professional liability insurance?" Professional liability insurance is purchased to indemnify designers for losses and costs involved in the defense of claims made against them.

Professional liability insurance covers claims arising out of errors, omissions, and negligent acts in the performance of professional design services. There are two types of coverage:

Claims made   A claims-made policy insures only against claims made during the period of the policy.

Occurrence   Occurrence coverage provides protection against claims occurring during the policy period, even if such claims arise long after the occurrence and the policy period.

It isn't necessary to become an expert in liability insurance. As with all other business considerations, you do need to be aware of the basics and apply common sense when making decisions. When you meet with a potential insurance agent, ask the following questions:

What will be insured under this policy?

What will not be insured under this policy?

Who is insured under this policy?

Where am I insured under this policy? (United States and Canada if applicable.)

What time frame is insured under this policy?

What is the limit of liability of this policy?

What are the insurance company's expectations of me as an insured?

How can I reduce my premiums?

What do I do if I think a claim will be made against me?

How can I become a better risk to the insurance company?

Many designers shy away from purchasing liability insurance because of the cost of the premiums. However, if you have expectations of designing larger work or public work, the purchase of professional liability insurance will become a necessity.

To some clients who hire designers, having professional liability insurance separates the heavyweights from the lightweights. These clients feel that having insurance shows stability as well as ability. Other clients give the impression that having liability insurance coverage is not important. They want the cheapest fee for the least expensive way to design the project. Theoretically, firms not covered by insurance will charge less for their services because their overhead is lower than that of firms with liability coverage. Look out, however, because some of those clients know what they are paying for, and others don't. Those who don't know may end up making a claim against you—even if you do not have insurance. The potential problems are costly and could even result in your bankruptcy! Paying the price for peace of mind and having coverage is the "right" way to go.

How do insurance companies figure premiums on professional liability insurance? They analyze your firm's practice by project type (residential design, stadiums, commercial design, institutional design, bridges, nuclear reactors, feasibility studies, private developers as clients vs. public clients, etc.). Further, they analyze the type of services that your firm offers (soil engineering, architecture, interior design, structural engineering, etc.) and its track record.

The insurance companies compare your firm's results with statistics on firms similar to yours, so that they can set the appropriate premium for accepting the risks of insuring your firm. Talk to your agent. Find out what other factors, if any, the insurance company considers in evaluating a design firm. Does the company have loss prevention programs for its insureds? Does it provide seminars and training? Does the company review contracts? How does it communicate current issues that face design professionals and their insurance coverage?

If you cannot afford insurance at this time, plan for it. Talk to an insurance carrier and get the facts. Plan to invest your profits into a policy after the first 12 or 18 months if possible. You will never regret it—if only for the peace of mind.

Look at it this way: In buying professional liability insurance, you have come to terms with the fact that eventually something will go wrong in your practice that will be out of your control. Having insurance protection will provide a reserve of money, set aside to help cover losses incurred by the event or judgment. Procuring professional liability insurance doesn't imply that you admit you are not perfect and will make big mistakes. It does send a signal to clients and other consulting design professionals that you care and have invested in risk management to protect your new asset, your firm, just as you protect your other assets in life.

Practicing Design Without Insurance

When many designers start their own firm, they decide to "go naked" and do without professional liability insurance for a period of time. If the degree of exposure is low owing to the nature of the practice (e.g., feasibility studies), this may be a viable alternative. Also, if you have few personal assets which cannot have a judgment placed against them, then personal bankruptcy is the potential outcome if a serious, real claim were made against you. Another alternative is to form a corporation without liability insurance or assets.

If you intend to practice design without professional liability insurance, *do* consult your attorney to maximize protection in your particular circumstances. What protects other colleagues may not protect you.

Buying professional design liability insurance is a business decision based on several factors:

- You need to evaluate the experience, technical competency, and quality control capabilities of yourself and your partner(s). Any weak characteristics in these areas will probably lead to a potential claim in the future.

- You need to evaluate your potential client base, and what kinds of clients they are. Will they sue you for claims made?

- You must evaluate the characteristics of your potential markets. For example, condominium associations are tough on the design profession because they are incorporated groups of people (not individuals) and they sue! Public-sector clients require liability insurance. Residential clients usually do not require liability insurance.

If your firm will be designing small projects, you may decide that not having insurance coverage is the right way to go. However, consider that you are not perfect, and that it is not a perfect world. You cannot, as a businessperson, ignore this fact. Eventually, according to Murphy's law, something will go wrong! Here are some options to consider if you elect not to purchase liability insurance:

- Set aside profits and fund an emergency reserve each month, each year. Make it an overhead expense of the firm. Put the money into a certificate of deposit so that it will be difficult to get at when you are tempted to meet other expenses. Be committed to the vision of this protection!
- Place all assets in your spouse's name or jointly in both your names (check your state laws) to make yourself more judgment-proof in the courts.

Finally, here are two options to consider when you do plan on purchasing insurance:

- Purchase low coverage.
- Purchase high deductibles. (Once you build your emergency reserve up to $25,000 or more, you will be better able to self-fund the deductible.)

Summary

Starting a new design firm is an exciting event in your life. Dealing with risk and eventually liability issues is part of business. Like it or not, you must make a decision on whether you will purchase liability insurance. Unfortunately for start-up firms, the insurance companies have the hammer. They don't know you. They don't know if you are a great designer or a bum! For an insurance company to take a risk on a new firm, the premiums must be worth its while. On average, insurance companies will charge up to 9 percent of gross revenues for new firms. For start-up sole proprietors, a premium of $6000 to $10,000 per year is a lot of money! The longer you remain in business, and the larger you grow, the premiums as a percentage of gross revenue decrease. Firms that have 5 to 19 employees pay approximately 4 to 5 percent of gross fees for premiums.

The bottom line is manage your risk and follow your gut feeling. If you have compelling reasons not to have liability coverage for a few years, do it—but be aware and careful. Always plan to purchase insurance in the future as your firm grows. Liability insurance is certainly a double-edged sword. For many firms, it is the fourth most expensive overhead item—behind payroll, health insurance, and rent. While most firms do not like paying for it, they also hope that they will never have to use it!

10
Office and Equipment Considerations

"When I had to make the decision on location, I remember having two important criteria. First, I refused to work at home, because home was an apartment—and I doubted I would be disciplined enough to work so close to the refrigerator and television. Second, I had to find an office that rented for less than my apartment. Why? I don't know, it just made me more comfortable, dealing with the risk of the lease.

I'll never forget paying that first rent check to my landlord. At first, I was very proud of this important event; however, as soon as I wrote the amount, I immediately thought of the next 23 checks I would be writing in the future. That is a lot of money! Can I afford to rent this office? Is it the correct image? Is the landlord going to clean the space properly? I have to write another one of these checks in 30 days. I sure hope some of my clients pay me beforehand!"

Where Is the Right Location for Your Firm?

How do you determine the "right" location for your new office? The first hurdle to jump is the *home office* vs. *outside the home office* dilemma. There is nothing more financially attractive than having an office in your home. The cost of the rent is right and the IRS allows you to write off part of the expense. It can be a real winner for some designers. A home office is convenient—you can roll right out of bed into the studio in a matter of minutes! No rush-hour traffic to deal with, no problems finding a parking space, no bad weather to fight! The home office saves travel time. (How many people do you know who travel more than an hour a day to the office? That's five or more potential billable hours per week if you work out of your home!)

Working at home is becoming a way of life for many business technology advances. As long as you have a phone, the world is your oyster! Armed with a phone, a fax machine, and a computer, you can do business anywhere in the world. Many designers who work out of their home say that they schedule all or a majority of their meetings at the client's office—not because they do not wish the client to see their office and its location but because clients appreciate the "level of service" of a designer who comes to them!

Working out of your home also has its disadvantages. One is image. Do you want to have your clients meet with you in your kitchen, or your office in the basement or on the second floor? For some practitioners, this is acceptable. For others, it poses an image problem. Another disadvantage of the home office is the presence of so many distractions—the refrigerator, the television, and so on. Finally, you need to check your local jurisdiction's zoning laws to see if a home office is permitted in your area.

To work out of your home requires discipline to help separate business from home life. You have to make the right decision for yourself and your new company—its vision and image. Some designers work out of their home for a period of time to develop a firm foundation for their new company, and then move onto office space outside the home. Other designers want to separate their office from their home at the outset, even though cost gets in the way. They forge ahead anyway, some with reckless abandon!

Many a designer overspends to outfit an office to obtain a particular image. Rome wasn't built in a day. Think before you act, and be reasonable in your approach to outfitting your new space. Chances are that you will schedule more of your client meetings outside your office than in it. Keep your fix-up costs simple in the beginning to portray a cost-conscious designer image, and invest your valuable capital on items that will make you profitable—staff, a computer, or other equipment.

Designers don't receive commissions because they have unique, wonderful offices. In a few years, when you are successful and grow, you will move on. Your tastes will change, and all that you invested in that trendy office will be out the window. Invest your money in your spatial needs wisely. Don't let your design ego get in the way!

Many designers have opportunities to locate their new, small quarters in a consultant's office, a contractor's office, or a developer's office building. Before you commit to any "opportunities" which may include free rent or bartered rent, consider the image of the location and whether it will give the impression that you are being "kept" and are not truly independent. Ask a colleague to evaluate the opportunity. Ask for advice. Only you can make the decision.

Some designers look for an office with complementary professional or business support capabilities. Essentially, you have your own office with your own furniture, but the rent expenses of the overall office and the receptionist's salary are shared on a proportional basis with all the tenants. Secretarial expenses are negotiated according to use. Usually, telephone answering services are available. If you do seek out a pooling arrangement, try to have a minimal notice period to end your lease. You may wish to leave because of expansion, inability to pay the rent, or personality conflicts. Make sure that the terms of your rental relationship are simple and in writing.

You can see how important a decision on office location is. For many, the decision is driven by economics at first. The funny thing about economics is that for as long as you are in business, you will wonder: "Can I afford to be located where I am? Is it the correct image? Does the space meet the company's vision?" It is an ongoing process!

How Do You Negotiate a Lease for Space?

Leasing space has its disadvantages, and it is important that you consult with your accountant and lawyer *before signing anything*. You should shop around for space before you negotiate—to make sure that you understand the market price and offerings and that you have the best arrangement for your needs. Leases generally have terms from one to five years. There are three types of lease payment formulas:

Net leases

Double net leases

Triple net leases

A net lease means that the base rent is the total rent. Double net is similar, except you must pay a pro rata share of any tax increase over the base tax period outlined in your lease. A triple net lease includes the rent, taxes, insurance, maintenance, repairs, improvements, management, and administration fees passed on by the landlord to the tenants.

Here are some tips on negotiating a lease:

1. Rather than negotiate a three-year lease, ask for a one-year lease with two additional one-year options. You minimize your risk if you can't pay or if you outgrow the space.

2. Consider offering the last two or three months' rent as a deposit. If you default the lease and leave before the end of the term, the deposit monies go to the landlord, and you are free of any further liability.

3. In a renter's market, try to get the landlord to pay for all your tenant improvements.

4. Ask for "free rent" terms in your lease to help offset start-up overhead costs.

5. Try to get out of paying the last month's security deposit rent, if possible. If not, get the landlord to pay you interest at a fixed rate for the term of the lease.

Equipping Your New Office

Now that you have made your commitment on office space, what will you need in the way of equipment to operate your new firm? The answer lies in how much equipment you presently own and how much money you have to spend.

Think about the firm that you just left. Does it have any old equipment that it would be willing to sell or give to you? To start out, make a list of the basics: telephone, drafting board, drafting equipment, reference material, lamps, conference table, typewriter/word processor/personal computer, office supplies, telephone answering machine and so on. Chart 15 presents an extensive list.

Each one of us is different. We have different backgrounds, priorities, and goals. The fact of the matter is that you can spend very little or thousands of dollars on start-up equipment. The decisions are hard, but be true to yourself. Delay the purchase of some equipment if you can, to spend the money saved on more important, less expensive equipment. For example, should you purchase or lease a photocopying machine when you start your firm? Would the $2000 to $4000 be better spent on another

CHART 15
Typical Business Equipment

Equipment	Cost Buy/lease	Present	Near future	Future
			Time frame	
Accounting software				
Adding machine/calculator				
Batteries				
Bookshelves for library				
Business cards				
CADD hardware				
CADD software				
CADD table				
Camera				
CD rom				
Chairs				
Coffeemaker				
Computer paper				
Computer printers				
Conference table				
Copy paper (8.5" × 11" and 11" × 17")				
Database software				
Desktop publishing software				
Dictation machine				
Drafting equipment				
Drafting table				
Electric eraser				
Envelopes				
Facsimile machine				
File cabinets				
Film				
Flashlight				
Flat files				
Floppy disk holder				
Folders				
Glue, rubber cement				
Label maker (Merlin/Kroy)				
Laptop computer				
Lamps				
Laser printer				
Letterhead				
Mailing labels				
Markers				

(Continued)

Equipment	Cost Buy/lease	Time frame		
		Present	Near future	Future
Mayline edge				
Mobile phone				
Modem				
Mouse				
PC computer				
Pager				
Palmtop organizer				
Paper clip holders				
Paper cutter				
Pencils				
Pencil holders				
Pencil sharpener				
Pens				
Post-it note pads				
Postage machine				
Phone				
Photocopier				
Scale for postage				
Scissors				
SF254/255 software				
Spray adhesive, spray mount				
Spreadsheet software				
Stapler				
Large stapler for drawings				
Tape/Scotch, double-coated, drafting				
Tape dispenser				
Tape measures (25' and 100')				
Tape recorder				
Telephone system				
Telephone answering machine				
Telephone message pads				
Three-hole punch				
Time management system				
Two-hole punch for files				
Typewriter				
White-out				
Word-processing software				

purchase if you could lease space in a building or an office with a photocopier next door that you can operate for 10 cents a copy? Must you purchase or lease a fax machine on the first day of your new business? Again, can you utilize the business fax next door for a while? Why spend the money!

Computerization

Do you need a computer on the first day of your business? The answer to this question depends on your generational position, your openmindedness to technological advances, and your literacy on the computer.

Computers are incredible helpers for small business as well as business in general. However, should you spend hundreds or thousands of dollars on accounting software if you are going to do only 20 projects and invoice $100,000 in the first year? Computers are constantly changing for the better. As soon as you purchase one, it is outdated! Remember, once you make a commitment to hardware and software, you must always upgrade to stay current with speed and accuracy.

If you plan to buy a computer, probably a personal computer (PC), you need to decide on the system platform you will operate on: Apple or DOS. For the millions of users in the world, Apple users swear by Apple, and DOS users swear by DOS. It is up to you, and the type of computer individual that you are. Both systems can operate software recommended for design firms.

Software applications for the start-up design firm should include word processing and spreadsheets at the minimum. You may consider incorporating an accounting software package as well. Be a smart shopper when it comes to computer hardware and software. Talk to your colleagues and find out what they recommend. Learn from their war stories, and try to avoid their mistakes. Many computer stores offer hardware with software already loaded on the harddrives. A variety of word-processing, spreadsheet, and accounting software exists, so be comfortable with your decision. Beware of software that is too complex for your new operation. For example, you do not need accounting software designed for a 50-person firm! It may be years before you get to that number. There is no status in overpaying! Purchase a system that will work for a firm of up to 20 staff.

Other software available for design firms include master specification formats, databases, desktop publishing, and CADD. If you have never been exposed to or worked on CADD, chances are that you won't need it to start your firm. If you have a background in CADD and are "one to one" (have extensive knowledge and experience and can work effectively on it), and if you can afford a CADD station with software and plotter, then go for it! The fact of the matter is that if you are not "one to one" on CADD when you start your firm, you won't have the time to be trained on it. Also, many designers purchase a CADD system but do not buy a plotter, to save money at the initial purchase. Their goal is to add the plotter later, and utilize a consultant's plotter or a reproduction house's plotter at present. Remember, there is a fair amount of risk involved in using another firm's hardware and plotters. The formats must be compatible, and you must coordinate your deadlines with their availability. If you can't afford a comprehensive PC CADD system, think twice before you act.

Another key decision is whether you should purchase a PC or a laptop platform to work from. Most businesses have conventional PCs in their offices. Laptops are the future of PCs, and are here now. New models appear almost daily, with faster and faster hard drives and memory. The benefit of a laptop is the transportability of the unit. You can work on it at home, in the office, on a train, in an airplane, or even in a client's office. Laptops offer the most flexibility. Some designers even have CADD on their laptops to make adjustments to files in the field, on a job site, or in the client's office. In the past, the computer lived in the office, and one may also have one at home. The laptop platform allows one to purchase one system and use it everywhere. PCs also have modems to link with other PCs and databases. Many designers use modems in their laptops when they travel to stay in touch with the office and data. Once again, before you make a purchase of a laptop or standard PC, talk with your friends and colleagues. Conduct your research, and help reduce your risk in making the right computer decision for yourself.

Once you decide to computerize, it takes a total commitment to remain up to date and be successful. A common complaint of small design firm owners is the expense of computerization. PCs for word-processing, spreadsheet, and accounting applications are affordable, but CADD-based PC systems are expensive. Since computers will become the backbone of the design profession by the year 2000, you might consider learning about software in an adult education course. Knowing how to format your correspondence and run a beginning accounting program will prove valuable.

Make your decision before you jump out of the airplane. Again, it will become increasingly difficult to get trained in computers after you have started the firm, since its operation will dominate your every waking moment. You will never regret making the commitment to computerization, because it will smooth your firm's growth transitions, speed your operations to make the firm more profitable, and in the big picture lead your firm more rapidly to success!

Telephone Equipment

The telephone is perhaps the single most important piece of equipment in an office! All of us take this simple late-nineteenth-century invention for granted. Today, not only can we talk over the telephone line, but we can transmit facsimile documents and also hook the telephone line up to our computers with a modem to obtain and transmit information. Since we live in the information age, the telephone will become more and more advanced and sophisticated in the business world. Just think of it. It wasn't long ago that "touch tone" phones were introduced, and today we call others from our cars, trains, and airplanes!

In selecting a telephone system, remember who you are—your firm's size—and be realistic in your search for the most important piece of equipment in your new office. Your phone system, whether it is a single phone or a system that can be expanded to 100 phones, is your direct connection to the outside business world. Make sure that the phone you buy is reliable and serviceable. If you start your firm in your home, you currently pay a monthly residential service charge for "unlimited" service. However, if you rent office space and start your firm in a commercial center, the phone company will charge you for each and every phone call that you place out from your office. You will notice this on your monthly bill. In the phone company's view, American business "pays the freight" for the cost of operating the telecommunications network in our country, and the residential consumer gets the "free ride." At first, you will feel compelled to keep track of how many calls you make daily, to check the phone company's computer accuracy. The sad news is that the computer is virtually infallible! Remember to get a great, reliable phone at first, and worry about expansion and those other "extra features" later. Investing in a "call waiting" system will save you money over buying another telephone line. Adding "call forwarding" will allow you to operate out of two separate areas, and give the impression of being totally accessible.

Finally, when you are just starting out and probably can't afford a receptionist, a telephone answering machine can be a life saver. Many of us claim that we hate talking to them but, let's face it, answering machines came of age in the 1980s and we cannot live without them, even in our homes! An alternative to an answering machine is a telephone answering service. These services are available just about everywhere, and offer a "real person" to answer your phone. After a while, however, your clients will notice that a different person answers your phone on different days, and that whenever "they" answer, you are *not* in. Many clients complain that these services are as impersonal as the notorious answering machine. Also, an answering service is a monthly expense, whereas an answering machine is a one-time expense. Finally, voice mail boxes may be offered by your local phone company with competitive rates. You make the recording, and you can access the messages anytime/anywhere. Contact your phone company for details.

Mobile Phones and Pagers

Many people who feel that accessibility is the key to success find the mobile (car) phone or pager the life saver of business. It is true that clients appreciate (and even demand) being able to reach you at a moment's notice. However, it is possible to be too accessible! If you give your pager number to clients, they expect a return phone call within minutes of their paging of you. Talk about expectations!

Manage your accessibility. Manage your clients' expectations!

If people despise telephone answering machines, they feel just as strongly about pagers going off in the middle of a meeting! It is true that pagers now come with varying options of alert, from a single beep to a vibration, to an annoyingly loud beep. Businesspeople who wear pagers do so for various reasons. Some refuse to delegate, and must be involved in every decision in their firm. Therefore, they want to be paged on any issue. If you are out of the office for great periods of time, and you have a secretary, a pager can be a great communications link. Some companies have codes that can be displayed on the pager screen to communicate the degree of importance of a beep. New units have the technology to print out messages on the small screen! Selecting a pager is a personal decision.

The car phone, "the business narcotic of the 1980s" is another technological breakthrough. It wasn't long ago that car phones were only for the affluent. Today, thousands of people enter into annual contracts for service on a daily basis. Phones that used to cost $4000 now sell for $100, and have more options and better reception! Car phones are the closest thing to being in two places at one time. Many users swear by them. Just think of being in transit to a meeting or marketing call, and having the ability to resolve an issue with a client, consultant, or fellow employee en route! Car phones save time and offer great accessibility.

Another advancement in mobile telecommunications is the hand-held portable cellular phone. These phones offer the maximum degree of accessibility. In the car, on the golf course, at the airport, walking down the street, you can be in touch with anyone.

Users advise against getting addicted to these new tools because of their expense. If a public phone or client's office phone is available, it is more prudent to use it at that particular point in time. How many businesspeople do you know who spend $700 per month on car phone bills? The time isn't inexpensive. Like other equipment decisions that you must make, approach the use of a car phone judiciously. Ration yourself so much time each day to control your costs. Think about every phone message. Can a return phone call wait till you get back to the office? Are the calls free or 10 cents vs. 50 cents a minute? Car phones, like computers, undergo rapid technological change. So if you want to purchase a phone, don't bother waiting for improvements. They occur every day! The time to purchase a car phone is the day you notice that, upon returning to your office, you cannot keep up with the calls you must return. There is nothing more frustrating than returning to your office to a "full" answering machine, or 10 telephone pink slips, with the clock reading five minutes to five! When the answering machine is full, how many calls did you miss? Returning 10 phone calls by five o'clock is impractical at best.

Your office telephone communications will grow naturally with the growth and success of your firm. Remember to keep a level head, and to base your decisions about equipment purchases on real need, not perceived need or ego!

Facsimile Machines

Facsimile (fax) machines barely existed in small business in the early 1980s. Today, they can be found in the smallest offices as well as in homes. Many large offices have multiple fax machines.

Fax machines are standard for business today in communicating details to consultants as well as contract to attorneys. Many clever businesspeople fax messages to the receiver rather than call, because they know that a written faxed message gets more attention than a telephone pink slip! By faxing a message or request, the ultimate delegation of a task has been accomplished.

Fax machines have raised clients' expectations about level of service. No longer can you negotiate more time with a task for a client by stating that you will express-mail a document for delivery tomorrow by 10 a.m. The client now expects a fax of the same document immediately! Be careful with this equipment. Do not allow your clients to enslave you to the fax machine.

When you purchase a fax machine, talk to your colleagues and confirm a good unit to purchase for a design firm. You need good resolution for detail transmissions. It is also highly recommended that you get a paper cutter for convenience and to save time. Another consideration is whether you want to purchase a unit that uses rolled fax paper, which is inexpensive but has a short file life, or one that produces the images on plain bond photocopy paper? There is a major cost difference between the two.

Facsimile communications are also available with PC computers, laptops, and some palmtop organizers. You can transmit information (paperless on the sending end) to a fax machine anywhere, and develop a paper copy at the receiving end. Software is on the market that is already formatted to incorporate your personalized information, along with interesting graphics to help read the information. Many, upon receipt of a fax in their office from a computer at the sending end, cannot believe the resolution. All you need is the software and a modem—and you can fax or electronic-mail (E-mail) to any fax machine or computer with a modem in the world!

Summary

We have examined many issues that you must consider and address in starting up your firm. Some designers find the number of issues overwhelming and decide not to start. Others overcome their intimidation by sharing their concerns with one or more partners.

As human beings, we start life learning to breath involuntarily. As we mature, we gain confidence in crawling, standing up, walking, running, driving, skiing. The more we do, the more confidence we gain. If we began worrying about every little thing that might go wrong, we wouldn't get out of bed in the morning! Starting a business is a similar journey. We may not do things right the first time, but as long as we learn from our mistakes, we will endure and succeed.

If you think you are the first person to face these issues, rest assured that you are not, and will not be, alone! Every person who founds an organization deals with the same uncertainties. If you try to handle multiple issues simultaneously, you will become confused and disenchanted. You must proceed in an organized, timely, logical, and practical fashion. Begin now to organize your thoughts as you plan your new venture.

PART 3

Getting Down to Business

11

Developing Preliminary Business and Marketing Plans

The secret of business is to know something that nobody else knows.

ARISTOTLE ONASSIS

What Is a Business Plan?

A business plan is a written summary of what you hope to accomplish by being in business and how you intend to organize your resources to meet your goals. It is an essential guide for operating your business successfully and measuring your progress along the way.

Why Prepare a Business Plan?

Starting and owning your own design firm isn't easy. There are no magic formulas or special buttons to push that can guarantee success. However, there are some fundamentals that give the entrepreneur designer a better chance of succeeding. One of the fundamentals is good planning.

Most designers prefer to be designers first and businesspeople second. However, planning and management skills are vital to business success. As in anything else in life, those who do not plan well run a very high risk of failure. If you do not know where you are going in your personal or your business life, there is little chance that you will arrive *anywhere* content and successful.

Developing a business is much like building a building. As designers, we know that a building will be successful only if its planning stages culminate in the "right" design that works for the client. Hundreds of decisions go into the building design. We are trained in design school and during our internship to build our ideas on a sound base and then, step by step, to develop a justified approach to a design solution. The "right" design doesn't occur on the first attempt, though most designers know that the first concept is often 90 percent "there."

Much like designing a building, establishing and operating a business requires hundreds of decisions. From day to day, a businessperson must develop a sound base, and step by step develop logical approaches to the challenges that everyday business life poses.

The most important aspect of a building is the construction of its foundation. The entire success of the project (will the building stand up?) depends on the foundation. Yet, after excavation, construction, and backfill, no one physically sees the foundation of the building. It is expected and taken for granted that the foundation will work. The "success" of the building is judged instead on its aesthetic value and function.

In business, people see you, your logo, and the product of your design, but they rarely see your business plan (your foundation). Other businesspeople—bankers, accountants, lawyers, and clients—fully expect that you have a business plan. Like a foundation, it is never seen, but it is taken for granted, because your firm should do a good job and succeed.

Planning the future forces you to think ahead with vision; it encourages realistic thinking instead of overoptimism. It helps you identify potential markets, income strategies and other competitive conditions that you will operate under. The great thing about developing a business plan is discovering new opportunities as well as weaknesses in your firm and your vision.

Having clear goals and a well-written business plan will help you make critical decisions and stay focused on your charted course. Your goals can always be altered—provided you have a documented business plan that enables you to evaluate the alternatives you will encounter day to day.

Write your plan with two purposes in mind:

1. The plan is a working document of how you are going to build your design firm.

2. The plan is also a sales document to bankers and clients, helping to communicate your vision and organizational skills.

A successful business plan achieves the following:

- It organizes objectives.

- It develops strategies for accomplishing those objectives.

- It sets priorities.

- It helps set schedules and timetables.

- It clarifies activities and delegates responsibilities.

- It anticipates problems.

- It creates solutions.

- It sets financial guidelines and goals.

Two out of three preliminary business plans ignore the first goal of organizing objectives. They therefore become weak selling tools for the businesses. Ten percent of ongoing business plans lose sight of the organizational goal and become instead complex, boring, unreadable documents that serve no purpose other than to be recycled!

Every large city has companies that specialize in writing business plans for firms. For a fee ranging from $1500 to $25,000 their experts will interview you, develop drafts for your review, and incorporate your comments into the final product. However, if you were to request five copies of "individual" plans developed by a particular firm, you would notice a sameness about them. The wording and clauses have the same ring, the ratios are always ideal, the graphics appear similar, the milestones overlap, and even the formats and covers look the same.

Your banker reads many business plans every year and can easily spot a "proposal company's" product. Such a formula plan is a signal that the firm hasn't taken the time to develop its own plan (no matter how much was spent for the proposal). The bank is likely to regard it as a pretext for borrowing money. Bankers rarely give a "processed" business plan much attention, because it is generic, impersonal, and homogenized.

It is critical, therefore, that you *write your plan yourself*. If you utilize another design firm's plan, you will become lazy in thinking about your own, and you may unthinkingly plagiarize wording, formats, and graphics. Force yourself to sit down and think about *your* goals and how you really are. You will be amazed at how easy the exercise becomes if you stick to a simple thinking and writing process.

When starting your firm, keep your business plan direct and to the point. You have a lifetime in business to refine, redefine, expand, and change your objectives. The preliminary plan should summarize your goals and objectives, and serve as an outline for a formal business plan. The preliminary plan is an abridged version, maybe 10 percent of the final's size. It is important, however, to address all the variables outlined in the recommended format below.

Format of the Business Plan

A business plan normally consists of five parts:

Introduction

The firm's concept

The firm's operation

The financial plan

Appendix

A business plan always starts with an *introduction*, a brief executive summary that captures the excitement of your new firm and attracts the immediate attention of the potential lender or client.

The *firm's concept* describes what your new design firm does, identifies your firm's market potential, and outlines your goals and action plan for the coming year. Make sure that your stated business goals are realistic, and in line with your financial goals, management ability, and personal and family considerations. The heart of the firm's concept is your monthly business forecast for the coming year. The business forecast forms the basis for your cash flow and projected income statement. It also assesses risks that you may encounter and outlines contingency plans.

The *firm's operation* summarizes your location (advantages and disadvantages), size (advantages and disadvantages), leasehold improvements, image and personality to be projected (and how you intend to do so), and hours of operation.

The *financial plan* outlines your present financial status and potential needs. This section should be brief, outlining your expected fees, costs, and profits for the year. The outline will serve as a benchmark for comparisons in the future.

Finally, the *appendix* should include items such as these:

Personal financial statement

Letters of intent from new clients

Summary of business insurance policies

Accounts receivable summary (if available)

Accounts payable summary (if available)

Summary of legal agreements

Copy of company brochure

List of references

Copies of news articles about the firm

Chart 16 presents a detailed checklist of points to be covered in your plan. Remember, formulating the plan is a cumulative process. Don't expect to isolate yourself, sit down, and in six hours bang out a complete plan. *Remember, grow into it!*

After reading all this, you may be saying to yourself, "My firm doesn't need a loan from a bank. I have my life savings to fall back on. I have an angel spouse and family with 'deep pockets' as a funding source, a safety net. I don't need a business plan, preliminary or final! Why take the time to write something that I know I will be doing my best at on a day-to-day basis? I can't predict the future anyway. I'm a designer, not a writer or businessperson!"

The fact of the matter is that simply thinking and writing down your ideas is half the battle! Even the shortest, most personalized business plan will gain respect from your banker. You may not need the bank's money now, but what about the future? Your private lending sources (safety nets) may change. Growth is a challenging process that devours cash. Assets such

CHART 16
Business Plan Checklist

I. Introduction

Company name

Address

Telephone number

Facsimile

Contact person

Paragraph about company
  Nature of design and market area

Financial needs
  Term loan, operating line of credit, mortgage, and so on

Summary of proposed use of funds

II. The Firm's Concept

Summary on one page
  Highlights/executive summary

Table of contents

Design profession outlook and growth potential

General markets

The competition

National and economic trends

Business goals
  One year
  Long term

Marketing plan
  Experience
  Target markets

Forecasts

>One month
>First year
>Long range

III.   The Firm's Operation

Location and space

Staffing required

Equipment required

Business structure

>Sole proprietorship
>Partnership
>Corporation

List of officers

List of contracts with clients

Background of key person(s)

Organization chart

Action plan

>Steps to accomplish this year's goals
>Schedule outlining checkpoints throughout year

IV.   The Financial Plan

Financial forecast

Preliminary balance sheet

Income and expense forecast statement

Cash flow forecast

Financing needs (if necessary)

>Loans

(Continued)

V. Appendix

List of references
  Banker
  Accountant
  Attorney
  Insurance agent
Personal net worth statement
Summary of business insurance coverage
Accounts receivable summary
Accounts payable summary
Legal agreements
Financial statements for company
Copy of company brochure
News articles on firm

---

as computers shouldn't be paid for in cash or out of cash flow. They should be financed—because of the tax advantages that such funding offers. Remember, business is a game. Most companies follow the same rules to achieve success. Eventually, your banker will become as important a player in the game as your accountant, lawyer, and insurance agent.

Imagine a contractor trying to construct a building without a set of plans and specifications! Now imagine trying to build a design firm without a business plan! *Do it!*

Sample Business Plan

Chart 17 presents a sample business plan for a design firm based on the outline presented in this chapter. Use the plan as a guide in developing your new firm's business plan.

What Is a Marketing Plan?

A marketing plan is a written summary of how you intend to market your firm. It is an essential guide for planning the future of the firm and

CHART 17
Sample Business Plan
Apple Architecture, Inc.
Architecture / Interior Design—Business Plan: 1994

I. Background

Company name	**Apple Architecture, Inc.**
Address	**401 Orchard Avenue** **Applegrove, Maryland 20000**
Telephone	**000-000-0000**
Facsimile	**000-000-0000**
Contact person	**George MacIntosh Apple IV, AIA** **President**

The Company

Apple Architecture, Inc. has provided quality architecture and interior design services throughout the Middle Atlantic region since 1981. The company was founded with a portfolio of mostly residential and small commercial projects. Through the 1980s, the firm strove to develop and maintain a commercial and institutional client base which expanded throughout the East Coast markets. With the expected downturn in the economy, the firm began concentrating in 1989 on developing a strong institutional client base, including government, health-care, and educational commissions. The company still maintains a strong residential design portfolio in the multifamily, single-family speculative, custom, and addition markets.

II. Business Concept

Outlook

The outlook of the architectural profession in the Middle Atlantic region is one of "steady no-growth." The current recession has hit the area,

(Continued)

with many firms downsizing. It has been said in the design industry that "the recovery is here," and that the business volume and size of a firm at present will be the size of the firm for the near future.

The small-scale residential design market is strong, along with institutional clients (health care, education, and government).

Apple Architecture, Inc. does not expect significant growth over the next year; however, after staff reductions in the past two years, we do expect to conduct limited staff increases in our CADD group.

The Competition

Apple Architecture, Inc., with a staff of 12, is considered in the profession as a "medium-sized" architectural firm. As of January 1993, 9 percent of the architectural firms nationwide are our size. Some 86 percent of the firms have fewer than 10 employees, and 5 percent have more than 20 staff positions. On a national basis, medium-sized firms control 17 percent of the market share of the gross billings.

The recession has created quite an erosion in the profession. Many of the larger firms have reduced staff, which has created many smaller, "one-person" firms.

Our firm has found that it is now competing with the start-up firms on smaller-scale projects. The "larger firms" are now competing for our "larger" projects, which is a challenge in and of itself.

We feel that we are in an excellent position because, given our size and experience, we can still compete on all levels and get "our share" of commissions. We have significantly reduced our overhead to compete with the competition and remain profitable.

Business Goals

Foremost, Apple Architecture, Inc. wants to be a *profitable*, service-driven design firm. We have managed our practice through the good as well as the difficult times over the past decade. What we have learned in the past 20 months has been how to control our cost of business and maintain a profit through the lean times.

Because of the economy and available developed structures, the construction industry will be heavily concentrated in the renovation and interiors markets over the next 5 to 10 years. We started our interiors division 5 years ago, expecting it to grow, to hedge our business in the lean "design" times ahead. The interiors work is profitable, and is helping open doors into the health-care industry. We expect our interiors group to make and possibly exceed the 30 percent volume of the firm by year end.

Our long-term business plan is to have an established design firm, noted for its quality service and commitment to the community and environment, and to be a leader of the profession in the Maryland marketplace. We see a similarity in the profession's future to that of the 1960s and 1970s, when there were not as many firms and most of the work was institutionally oriented.

Apple Architecture, Inc. has been in a survival mode over the past year; however, we do see a brighter future, unlike the 1980s, with more stable and rewarding times through community-oriented projects. The role of designers will increase as problem solvers to government and society during the challenging decade of the 1990s. We at Apple Architecture, Inc. are proud to be in our "position."

Forecasts

Apple Architecture, Inc. enjoyed its highest-gross volume year in 1992. We concentrated on reducing our overhead throughout the year, and invested our profits into reducing our payables to consulting engineers and vendors.

The first half of 1993 has been challenging; however, owing to our decreased operational costs, we have been profitable.

Our current workload and contracts include the following:
Apple Hill Elementary School addition for Apple County
Apple County Public Safety Headquarters
These should result in a $1 to $1.2 million gross volume year, down from $1.4 million in 1992.

III. Business Operation

Location

Apple Architecture, Inc. operates its business from a 6000-gross-square-foot office building located at 401 Orchard Avenue, Applegrove, Maryland. This central Apple County location provides our firm with un-

(Continued)

paralleled access to our client base in Apple City, Apple County, MacIntosh County, and Winesap County. We have easy access to the interstate highway system for providing service throughout the state.

Staff

Apple Architecture, Inc. currently has a staff of 12. Of the number 5 are licensed architects. Please refer to our corporate background for further detailed information.

Business Structure

Apple Architecture, Inc. has been a corporation since 1986.
Officers:

George M. Apple IV, AIA	President/ Treasurer
John Granny Smith, AIA	Vice President
Denise B. Apple	Secretary

measuring its progress. Writing a marketing plan is not difficult. As a matter of fact, the most difficult task is sitting yourself down and doing it!

Why Prepare a Marketing Plan?

If you polled 100 design firms in the United States today, fewer than 20 would have a documented marketing plan. And probably half of those firms haven't updated their plans in over a year.

So, why prepare a plan? As with the preliminary business plan, it is important to focus on your thoughts and visions, and document them. Don't be scared, and don't think that once you document your ideas, they cannot change. Having clear marketing objectives will help you make critical decisions and stay focused on your charted course of business. As with the business plan, there are two goals to keep in mind:

1. Keep the marketing plan simple. It is a working document which must be flexible to allow for change.

2. The plan is also a sales document to bankers and clients, communicating your vision and organizational skills.

CHART 18
Sample Marketing Plan
Apple Architecture, Inc.
Architecture / Interior Design—Marketing Plan: 1994

Mission Statement

Apple Architecture, Inc. will continually strive to expand its capabilities to perform larger-scale projects in the commercial, educational, and institutional markets while broadening its image publicly as a reputable, problem-solving design firm.

Situation Analysis

After a decade of developing a comfortable commercial and residential client base, the firm began in 1992 to take on a broader range of larger-scale educational and institutional design work including religious and federal government (Corps of Engineers) work.

A direction was established to concentrate on local health-care institutions, public schools, and local, state, and federal government clients. Both the architecture and interior design marketing efforts will concentrate on these markets.

Goals/Strategies/Time Frame

1. Become a better-known architecture/interior design firm

2. Increase interior design services to 30 percent of business volume by January 1994

3. Obtain short list/interview for public school project

4. Obtain a public school design project

5. Obtain a major health-care design project

6. Maintain religious design work

(Continued)

7. Maintain and expand corps of engineers work

8. Concentrate on obtaining open-end contracts with local, state, and federal clients

9. Maintain level of new residential as well as additional commissions—in light of the economy and low interest rates

10. Expand community college design work

Format of the Marketing Plan

A preliminary marketing plan normally consists of three parts:

- Mission statement
- Situation analysis
- Goals/strategies/time frame

The plan starts with the firm's *mission statement*. Keep it simple, and under 35 words! This paragraph summarizes the who, why, and what you are.

The *situation analysis* is a written "snapshot" of where the firm is now and where it has been.

The *goals/strategies/time frame* section deals with just that: your stated goals, the strategies you plan to implement to obtain the goals, and the time frame in which you plan to accomplish your goals. This section provides a benchmark for measuring your success.

Sample Marketing Plan

Chart 18 presents a sample marketing plan for a design firm based on the outline presented in this chapter. Use the plan as a guide in developing your new firm's marketing plan.

Summary

Starting and operating a design firm requires flexibility not only from the owner but also from the firm's business and marketing plans. Think simple thoughts, document simple strategies and goals, and provide yourself with a simple framework for success! Read your marketing and business plans at least once a week, if not once a day! Remind yourself of who you are and why you are doing what you are doing. If you feel different about an issue, document the change and continue on with your business. Join the less than 20 percent of design firms that have well-thought-out, documented plans. They are the ones that enjoy success, while the balance sit back and wonder why.

Do yourself a favor. Spend the few hours necessary to develop the ideas necessary for your plans. You will never regret the time spent!

12
Fear, Risk, and Guilt

Always do what you are afraid to do.
RALPH WALDO EMERSON

*Only those who dare to fail greatly can ever
achieve greatly.* ROBERT KENNEDY

*There is no security on this earth, only
opportunity.* DOUGLAS MACARTHUR

*No one understands the life, trials, and tribulations of the
founding entrepreneurial businessperson! Your family, friends,
and clients do not want to hear about your problems, because
they don't think that you have any! You have your own
business, so you must be successful! You even find it difficult to
discuss your feelings with your full-time part-time employees,
because they will probably not understand. Why is it that,
when I do confide in others, the answers they give me don't
make sense? Boy, it is lonely here at the top of my business!*

Just as you become comfortable with the "milestone" goal of having your own firm—of not having to listen to anyone else, of being able to run the show—this book comes along and informs you of the hundreds of considerations that come into play, making the decision that much harder and more frightening! Many designers get right to the point of putting on their parachutes, but then—after talking with colleagues or reading a book like this—they refuse to "jump out of the airplane" because of their fear of failure and rejection.

The reality of it is that all designers who have started their own firms—those who have been successful as well as those who haven't—have experienced the same fear. It is normal. Anyone who says that he or she was confident from the moment of starting out, and has never had a single worry since, is flat-out lying!

Running a design firm is a challenge. Especially scary is running a business without any formal training or business plan. It is much like dealing with the unknown.

What Is Fear?

Fear is anxiety caused by real or imagined danger or pain. It is apprehension or concern for one's well-being.

Doubt is natural to every human being, young and old, inexperienced or experienced. We all have our limitations. Wiping doubt out of our minds is a technique we all need to learn. Every challenge that we face every day requires a decision. If doubt exists, decisions will not be made, and if they are, the odds are that they will be erroneous.

Many people are fearful about issues that they cannot control. It is human to feel this way. However, in business, there are so many things you can't control, that you need to develop a positive mindset:

Determine what you are capable of changing, and do it. Accept what you have no control over changing, and do not try.

Why worry about issues that you cannot control? Suppose you are given the opportunity to present your new firm's qualifications in a personal interview for a major project. Suddenly, the potential client takes ill and asks to reschedule the appointment. Further, the client calls on Friday and promises to call back the following Monday. This event will set many businesspeople "off" in hundreds of ways—to doubting the situation, developing fear, and worrying until the prospect calls! Some will begin to worry that the client has already made a decision and is not telling the truth. Others, having prepared extensively, will lose their momentum and interest. Still others will wonder if a competitor's interviews went overtime and extremely well.

You must be able to separate your emotional and intellectual feelings on an issue. Sure, emotionally you may be concerned about the client's canceling your interview. However, intellectually your realize you have no control over the situation—so why worry about it? Spend the time you now have open in your afternoon schedule to deal productively with other issues in the firm.

Fear is packaged two ways in life: *real fear* and *imagined fear*. The example used above illustrates imagined fear. Real fear is when you need "that" check from your client to make ends meet. You call the client, talk it over, and agree to drive to the client's office to pick the check up personally. Then, when you get there, you discover the client had to leave because of an emergency and didn't sign "that" check for you. This is the sort of real fear you will experience.

People react to fear because they are afraid of making mistakes, being a failure, and being subject to rejection. Many do not even attempt to take on challenges because of their fear of not succeeding and being subject to ridicule. How many intern designers do you know who are so scared of the professional registration exam that they cannot even find the nerve to take it?

Fear is an emotion that lives with each and every one of us, every day, and will continue to live with us to our grave. Whether it is passing that test, catching that airplane, getting that job, convincing that client, or having that baby, we will always show concern over events in our lives. Believe it or not, some people have fear of success, and of the potential life that will be associated with their success!

You must learn to view fear positively, as the pulse or alternator in your daily life. Every business, from the largest corporation to the smallest one-person design firm, deals with the same concerns and issues, and fear exists in every mind involved. Sure, you can worry about cash flow right along with General Motors. Come to think of it, if you really concentrate, you can imagine that none of your clients will pay you over the next 60 days, and you will go into bankruptcy! What you need to do is take that fear of not being paid (which is imagined fear) and turn it around. Use the emotional energy created to physically call the clients and manage the accounts. Another fear common to all designers is where the next commission will come from. Don't waste time worrying about this issue! Exhibit a positive attitude. Feel confident that the next lead is right around the corner and that you will take it on successfully.

Manipulating fear like an alternator in an automobile makes fear work for you. It keeps you alive with a motivating charge, sparking your activity toward success.

Fear will diminish when you deal with an issue the second time, having learned from the first experience. Also, when you establish "inchpebbles," you break the fear down into manageable little pieces, and emotionally you can deal with smaller challenges more easily. It is like getting on a bike for the first time in 30 years. You take it for granted that you will ride that bike. And you do. It is amazing how few of us encounter fear in that experience!

What Is Risk?

Risk is exposure to the chance of injury or loss; it is a hazard or dangerous chance.

Risk as a whole is a disagreeable idea to most people. It is commonly viewed as a negative. Taking risks always implies taking responsibility. People shy away from risk; they prefer to be free from choice and responsibility. They are afraid of failure. However, there would be no risk without the possibility of failure.

Most people avoid taking risks in the pursuit of gains in life; however, they will choose risks to avoid sure losses. The lesson here is that when faced with certain failure, people do embrace risk; therefore, they are not really averse to risk. They are averse to loss and failure. Resisting risk, and the change it involves, often stems from a fear of appearing stupid. Risk takers, however, usually do things contrary to the norm, and may often be wrong. But being wrong can be part of the process. Didn't your parents tell you to learn from your mistakes?

Learning from the Past

Risk takers point out that risk is a process of trial and error. It is impossible to be perfect; therefore, one will always make mistakes and experience failure. Failure is a far better teacher of life than success, because the lessons learned from failure are more poignant!

In business, very little is predictable. Business can be challenging. It doesn't occur in straight lines, nor is it smooth. Businesspeople have learned over time that to survive in a business enterprise, they must modify and even disrupt old ways of doing things and create new ways. In business, as in life, only change is constant. Many fear change because of uncertainty. Change requires taking risks. Risk taking sometimes results in failure, but only taking risk produces progress and profits.

In business, risk is the agent of change that prevent firms from becoming stagnant. All businesses experience change and risk taking. Usually, taking risks works, but sometimes it doesn't. The only certainty is that if a company resists change and risks, it will eventually fail.

Think about the older principals in your current or former firm. This comment probably sounds familiar: "That's not the way we do things around here! We know better, because we've been doing design this way for 20 years! We are experienced, so don't challenge it!" One major lesson to learn about taking risks in business is to not guide your decisions on past performance. You must be innovative and look into the uncertain future.

Looking to the Future

The art of forecasting for business, like predicting the weather, is not perfect. Nor is being human perfect. As a business owner, you must be flexible in your day-to-day business activity. If something doesn't work, try something else. Developing a flexible approach will help make you take greater risks in the future. Business in the 1990s can no longer depend on stable service life cycles. Consider this analogy:

> In the past, running a business was like paddling a canoe on a lake with the water surface like glass. You identified your target (destination), and you glided through the smooth water, in a straight line to your goal. The fact was that if you concentrated and didn't deviate from your course, you would reach your target successfully.
>
> Running a business in the 1990s is like having the same canoe, but this time you have put into a white water river! The target is visible; however, you will probably have to change course, fight challenging currents, flip upside down, and adjust the direction of your course many times to reach the goal!

Classic entrepreneurs don't take on risk because they love danger. They take on risk because they know that only through risk will they find true value. If entrepreneurs didn't accept risk, enterprise and innovation would not be accomplished. Risk takers create action out of inaction.

Change is unending in business and life. It is uncertain and infinite. Therefore, risk taking must be a continuous process in your daily life. The key to deciding to take on risk is to develop a sense of the *degree* of a risk. You need to adjust your attitude toward it, and learn to live with it. Take on risk intentionally rather than accepting it. Risk taking is an investment in your new firm's future!

What Is Guilt?

Guilt can be described as a feeling of responsibility or remorse for some offense or wrongdoing, whether real or imagined.

Guilt is a major trait in businesspeople that fosters fear! Guilt can be a positive trait when you know that you are not being fair to yourself. You will find it easy to spread guilt and share it with others when you have started your firm. Be careful!

One side effect in developing good work habits is developing a business conscience. A conscience is a way of turning guilt around. Having that eighth sense, that of a business conscience, will help you manage and guide your firm through the white water of the business environment. It will aid you in taking risks and in making value judgments and decisions. A conscience will keep you honest and fair and gain you and your firm respect from others. It is a quality that most people admire, and will help you to achieve success through referrals, because clients like you and your firm for what they stand for.

Having and practicing a business conscience can be frustrating and a challenge to your patience. Maintain a positive attitude and keep guilt in check. A little guilt is good for a new business. You will be amazed at the impact you will have not only on yourself but on your firm and the people who surround you.

Managing Risk, Fear, and Guilt

Every day you will be required to manage risk, fear, and guilt. Every decision that you make, from the moment you choose to get up in the morning to that late-night moment you decide to "call it quits for the day," will have risk associated with it. Your experience in similar situations and your ability to deal with fear in unfamiliar areas will determine your success.

Remember, no human is perfect. However, successful people make the "right" decision *most of the time*. If you face a challenge that tests your experience or throws off your sense of direction, ask a mentor, colleague, or friend to "partner" with you in making that decision.

A major criticism leveled at designers is that their goal in practice and in life is to be "published." Big deal! There is more to life than having your creation documented in a magazine—to be used to dress up your promotional literature, gain accolades from your colleagues, and stroke your ego! The best way to manage fear, risk, and guilt is to set goals and remain focused on them. Success is built on good work habits, routines, and goals.

You will find it easier to handle the challenges surrounding your new firm if you balance priorities and set routines:

1. Your new firm isn't the only entity in your life. Family, friends, and social life are just as important! Try to develop a balance among all your interests.

2. Get organized and set goals—small, medium, and large.

3. Normalize your work habits:

   Arrive at your office every morning at the same time.
   Attempt to eat lunch at the same time every day.
   Eat breakfast every morning.
   Plan the use of the prime time of your practice (8 a.m. to 5 p.m.) with great care; this is the normal time that clients, vendors, and other businesses operate.

4. Take one day of the week off to recharge your batteries.

5. Limit your workday to 16 hours.

6. Get a reasonable amount of sleep each evening.

7. Pace yourself.

8. Plan the events of each new workweek on Sunday evening.

9. Start Monday morning with the proper attitude.

10. Set appointments with yourself to study and deal with administrative issues.

11. Market, market, market.

12. Perform as many production-oriented tasks outside of prime business hours as possible.

13. Turn on the answering machine during the day.

14. Take a "quiet hour" in the evening and turn on the answering machine to help separate yourself from others.

Once you start your firm, you will see how easy it is to work 16 to 20 hours per day! You don't physically have to be at the office or with a client to be working. Your mind will start working when you awake in the morning, while you take your shower, on the commute to the office, through lunch, on the commute to a meeting, on the way home, during and after dinner, even as you lie in bed awaiting sleep.

If you allow yourself to become a time clock, you will be successful, but successful in only one aspect of life. There is more to life than work, career, and profession! Truly successful entrepreneurial designers are able to develop a critical balance among business, family, and profession. Developing and maintaining that balance will provide a richer, healthier, and more fulfilling life.

Refining Your Daily Routine

In your daily routine, it is important to establish small, obtainable goals—the inchpebbles referred to throughout this book. Simple goals, to obtain on a daily basis, may include not only waking up at 6 a.m. but getting out of bed at 6 a.m.! Simple goals in business include starting your day consistently at 8 a.m., making two marketing cold calls per day, designing your projects in the morning when you are rested and fresh, and conducting administrative and marketing functions in the afternoon when most of your clients are in their offices, out of meetings, and available to communicate with. Long-range goals—milestones in the journey to success—are visionary and need to be the sum of many inchpebbles.

Set a deadline for every task that you assign yourself! When you receive a commission for a project, establish a schedule and determine the various deadlines needed to accomplish work that meets your client's expectations. You will be amazed at how impressed clients will be with your sense of care and organization if you state, after accepting a commission, that you would like to discuss the target dates for *all* the project's phases or tasks and tentatively commit your time and theirs to those specific dates.

Being deadline oriented makes you appear and become disciplined. You will be more productive and better organized; you will appear more logical. Most important, you will reek of accountability, responsibility, and success! Clients appreciate these qualities in designers and consultants, because it assures them that they have made a right decision, and it makes *them* look good!

Remember, you need to establish daily work goals—specific ends that you strive for—in order to appear to be and to be successful. Further, you need to develop the deadline orientation necessary to compete in today's business climate. The way to manage your time, work goals, and daily routine is to practice a sound time management system that works for you.

The Value of a Time Management System

The simplest, most fundamental thing you can do first is to purchase a time management system to help you organize your time and daily "things to do." Further, this device will give you a method to schedule periodic reviews, deadlines, and anniversaries and to record long-range ideas and observations.

Many designers utilize the "daytimer" or "week at a glance" system to assist them in keeping track of their lives as well as their company's. Another benefit of keeping such a daily diary is that it gives you a detailed record of your day-to-day activity to look back on and learn from—and then to set new goals based on your experiences.

Another popular technological advancement is the "pocket wizard"—a calculator-sized microprocessor that records your schedule and activities. Some systems can be interfaced with a PC for convenience and expandability. Information can be shared with your secretary's PC so that your office also has your schedule and can print out a hard copy as backup if necessary. As with computers in general, technology evolves every day and renders yesterday's pocket creations obsolete.

In order to be successful in operating your business, you will need to meet more and greater challenges every day. Learn not to depend on your memory for all scheduled events. Few people have the ability to retain so much information. Remember the idea of scheduled events, and let your written diary or computer organizer retain the details. Learn to depend on it.

Your time management system is your best friend in planning the future, and in documenting a present that is soon to be the past. If you are effective and consistent with good recording habits, your time management system will help you achieve success much quicker than you ever imagined.

There Are Only 168 Hours in a Week!

Manage your time. Next to your ideas and creativity, it is the most sacred commodity in business. Remember, there are only 168 hours in a week. That's all; there is no chance of adding any more!

Let's be analytical about this. Think about those 168 hours. Most of us need an average of 7 hours of sleep per day (49 hours per week, or 28 percent of our time!) Another 40 hours (33 percent) are prime business hours: M–F 8–5.

The secret of success is how you manage the remaining 79 hours.

In your first year of business, you will feel that it is necessary to work at least 80 hours per week, which leaves a precious 39 hours to commute, eat, work around the house, and relax! Is that enough? These time constraints make it essential to maintain a balance among the business, personal, professional, and family requirements in your life. Learn not to be emotional and develop workaholic traits. Look at your 168 hours objectively at first, then subjectively in planning them. You will learn that each one is precious! Never in your life has every single hour of every single week been so important!

The interesting thing is that if you spend too much time in one area of your life, the other areas begin to suffer. Stress and discontent result. Learn to read the signs in your family, friends, and colleagues, and in yourself! Your relationships and health can be at risk if you do not effectively manage your life and time, and give each their fair due. No one wants to be treated as important only part of the time. You need to "partner" the various areas of your life and develop a way of getting them to work in concert with one another. No one area is more important than another. All are equal in value because they are interdependent. Clients depend on your business, the business depends on you, and your family depends on you, your business, and your clients. It all goes round and round!

Summary

Goal setting is an ongoing exercise. As in your design practice, set the easy, obtainable goals first to gain confidence and develop momentum. This will help you set and obtain the more complex goals later.

Challenge yourself! Set goals, both milestones and inchpebbles, and you will be amazed at how quickly you obtain results. Use time management techniques to help maintain a critical balance among the various areas of your life (family, friends, business, profession, community) and to partner them into one concerted effort toward success.

Manage fear, risk, and guilt (your business conscience) by dealing successfully with inchpebbles, and evaluate your progress in quarterly and annual reviews. You will be surprised at how taking the time to study past facts and events will give you the confidence and experience you need to meet future challenges head on!

13
Success

Success is not so much what you are, as what you appear to be.　　ANONYMOUS

You always pass failure on the way to success.　　MICKEY ROONEY

I'll never forget getting that first large contract. My goal in my first year was to have $30,000 under contract. The project called for performing construction administration services for only seven months and was valued at $6000! Imagine, this one contract was 20 percent of my yearly goal, and it came into my life out of nowhere! That night, my wife and I celebrated with a major dinner and an incredible bottle of wine. Now that made it all worthwhile!

Seeing my name on my personal checks throughout college was no big deal. However, the first time I prepared and cut a check with my new firm's name on it was a significant event in my life! I thought to myself, 'Isn't this check and the company name impressive? This check has value, it is important. Boy am I impressed!' I first felt pride of ownership when I left my new office on my first day of business. When I closed the door behind me, I felt the most incredible sense of accomplishment, like none that I have ever experienced!

What Is Success?

Success is having a favorable result (wealth, fame, or any other outcome) turn out the way it was hoped for.

In business, both success and excellence tend to be measured in ways that can be quantified. Others have said that success is measured over time. In design, however, success is not so clearly defined, because there is no single definition of it and there is no one formula for achieving it.

The target of goal setting, whether inchpebbles or milestones, is success.

Success begins with the proper attitude, and starts with you! Developing a "victorious attitude" assumes from the very beginning that in all you do, you are going to come out on top. Try it! From the moment that you awake in the morning until you complete that last design decision late at night, be confident and communicate it to others through your body language as well as your attitude and verbal communications.

Isn't it human nature to have ups and downs? How can you be "up" all day? The answer lies in how you approach your challenges and act when encountering others. Be a salesperson all day. When you talk to your client, banker, or lawyer, have an upbeat, confident, victorious attitude. Be assured. Confidence is catching! When people encounter someone who exhibits the above characteristics, they believe that the person is successful and want to associate themselves with that person. Think about it. People want to deal with successful people. This is why some are attracted to celebrities, and others are attracted to a successful person's expertise.

Clients want to deal with successful design firms because they want to get value for their money and design product. Dealing with a successful designer brings notoriety and peace of mind that the professional is responsible and accountable and will design a building that meets the client's expectations.

Your banker wants to deal with a successful designer for two obvious reasons. First, if you have been granted a loan from the bank, your banker wants you to succeed so you can pay back the principal and most importantly the interest on the loan. That is one of the reasons banks exist: to make money on business. Second, your banker wants you to succeed because chances are that if you design well and service clients well, your firm will grow and prosper and have more money needs. Guess who has all the money for your needs?

Your attorney wants you to be successful so that he or she won't have to represent you in court over any issue. The attorney would rather help you develop contracts and form the business, and give you advice on day-to-day operations and how the law affects your decisions. A good client for an attorney will start as a sole proprietor and grow into a partnership or corporation. There is plenty of work for the lawyer to do in refining your forms of business and reviewing your leases as you shift to new quarters because of the need for space to handle all your new employees.

Your accountant wants you to be successful because it is her or his job to document your business activity and give you advice on present and future challenges. Accountants are wizards with numbers. They can make an average year look great! As your business becomes more and more successful, you will need more services from your accountant. In the beginning, the accountant may generate your income statement and balance sheets. Later on, you may develop trial statements for accounting review and approval before submission to your lender.

The longer you are in business, the more challenges you will encounter and the more experience you will gain. Successful designers are not just the ones who get published in the magazines. They are the principals of firms who have survived—staying in business for one, two, three, four, or more years. Sure, many designers poor-mouth their journey in business. That is their problem. That is the inspiration behind this book. The fact of the matter is that most of our colleagues do a poor job of running their firms. They don't have the formal business training or the initiative to plan. They want to be designers first, designing design, and let the business fall as it may.

Ingredients for Entrepreneurial Success

Before you start your firm, know yourself. You need to exploit your strengths and develop your weaknesses to obtain success. Cultivate and utilize them. If you are good in design, take that for granted and concentrate on your administration, production, marketing, and financial skills. Many firms are founded with three to four partners, each wanting to design, but each one also specializing in one of the other four areas of the practice. Set your inchpebble and milestone goals, achieve them, and be successful!

The following are essential ingredients for entrepreneurial success.

1. Successful designers have clear, definable goals. *Always.* Designers who wander here and there usually do not succeed.

2. You have to care passionately about your design and your service to clients. You have to care so much that you will defend your design to anyone, at any time, in any place—enough so that you will strain your relationship with friends and family because they will grow tired of hearing about it.

3. As a designer, you must persevere. Listen to that small, stubborn voice that says, "I'm not going to give up. I don't care what you say or think!"

4. You need to be prepared. This book has attempted to give you some idea of what you will encounter. Do your homework!

5. You must maintain perspective. This is what will keep you from going insane during the entire process. When you are afraid of failure, perspective will remind you that failure isn't fatal, and the business is not the only variable in your life. Other things matter as well. Perspective will also keep you from getting a swelled head if you are successful.

6. You need to perform. Your dreams and vision are very important when you own your own firm; however, they do not take the place of getting the job done! As a designer, you have to motivate yourself to do the work—because there is no boss over you. You are it!

7. You must have presence! In business, presence is the ability to hold clients' attention when you are with them and be remembered by them when you are not.

Summary

Remember that success is not a destination, it is a journey. Now that you are on your journey, what exactly lies out there in the future?

14
The Future

After my first year in practice, my wife and I took a trip to
Greece to visit friends and see the beginnings of Western
architecture. Having lived with myself for a year with 16-hour
days, six days a week, completely saturated with my business,
I will never forget the most humbling experience of my entire
life. There I was, standing on the Acropolis, thinking the entire
world was centered back in the office that I left behind, 7500
miles away, and not one person within 100 feet of me was
speaking English, and no one could have cared less that I was
an architect with the most important practice in the world 7500
miles away! That really put my life, business, and future in
perspective.

Darling, you are working so many hours overtime. I haven't
seen much of you, and the kids have forgotten who you are!
You are wearing yourself down, and I worry about you!
Working too hard can be unhealthy, and if you drop dead, I will
kill you!

Now that you have started on your new adventure in life, you can expect to encounter the ultimate challenges and thrills associated with developing, cultivating, and growing a new business enterprise: *your design firm!* You have embarked on the most rewarding and most frustrating exercise of your life. Maintaining a balance in the firm's organization and operation while being profitable is a difficult challenge!

As a firm owner, you will face different challenges every minute, every hour, every day, every month, every year! You will encounter several changes in your personal life, and several business cycles during your lifetime. Risk, change, fear, and success run hand in hand for the business owner.

The Three Faces of Ownership

Thousands of designers leave the companies they work for each year in order to start their own firms. Most of them have a fuzzy idea (blurred vision) of growing their practice into a thriving, well-recognized firm. Growth is almost always a goal for designers. Should you decide that growth is for you and your firm, you can expect to experience the following role changes in the future:

First person   Owner/founder

Second person   Owner/manager

Third person   Chief executive officer

First person.   Owner/Founder

Once you have started your firm, you are the owner and totally responsible for its success. You do it all. You certainly have pride in yourself and your design product, and feel independent. You provide a high level of personalized service to your clients, since you control and do all of the design product.

As we have discussed, however, there are limitations on you and your new start-up firm if you do not grow. First of all, there is not enough of "you" to go around once you take on multiple projects. Further, if you have no staff, there is no backup. Frustration may set in because you will feel like you are running the business more than designing, and are out of control of your destiny.

You have reached a decision point. Should you grow? Do you take on one or more partners or add staff? If you elect to grow, you enter the next stage of your individual business development: the second person.

Second Person. Owner/Manager

If you felt frustrated during your first-person experience, you can welcome an entire new set of rules and issues to add to your frustration! Since you decided that there is not enough of you to go around, you have added a partner or staff. Now you must learn to manage not only the firm but other people! As a designer, you were trained to design, not manage firms and people. So how do you manage people to think like you because everyone who retains your services wants you, right? Wrong! You must develop people skills and effectively manage your staff or partner to turn out a consistent, successful design product.

Consider the story of a talented carpenter's apprentice who, once qualified, left the firm and started his own carpentry subcontracting company. He framed a house, then another, then another, and the word got out that this particular carpenter was good, very good. Soon he had more projects than he knew what to do with! He had to make a decision: to turn work down or to hire carpenters who, in his view, were not as good as he was and then assume a new role of monitoring their work and producing a consistent product. The great carpenter became a great manager.

This is a very important stage in your professional career. Many design professionals cannot manage people. They can manage clients and projects, but not employees! You need to decide whether you can delegate the responsibility necessary to grow. Growth isn't for everyone. Many professionals experience unsuccessful growth, in that they cannot delegate authority well and cannot share control and ownership well. As a result, they lose good, experienced staff.

This second-person stage can go on for the rest of your career. However, should you decide to seek the next plateau, you will be the manager of managers in your firm, or the chief executive officer.

Third Person. Chief Executive Officer

At the third-person stage in your career, you will focus on the management of the business and make decisions on the firm's direction, consider branch offices and mergers, and think about expanding the firm to other design disciplines.

Few designers get to this stage of a business, since their firms are generally small concerns with staff of 40 or less. Interestingly, the more staff and managers that you control, the more income you will command.

You will most probably encounter the first- and second-person experiences within the first few years of your new firm. The third person is saved for the select few who are cut out for that particular challenge.

Business Life Cycles

Like people, firms age. As newborns, they enter an introductory stage. As adolescents, a growth stage. As adults, a maturity stage. And if careful planning isn't exercised, they enter a decline stage leading to their demise. These are the life-cycle stages that the majority of businesses experience.

Introductory Stage

The introductory stage, like infancy, is the riskiest of the four. If your commissions are viable, and if you manage your firm's vital signs well and have a little luck, at the end of your first year in business you will be in the black rather than in the red. If you continue to monitor the vital signs and keep tight reins on your firm's spending, you will maintain profitability month to month, and develop the necessary cash to fuel your firm's growth. As business volume grows, you will gradually need part-time help and eventually full-time employees.

Use common sense and set your sights on a goal to add staff, whether administrative or technical, during the first year. Keep ploughing your profits back into the firm's operations to maintain a steady climb. You will be surprised at the results if you focus on your vision, even if you are attempting to "just survive."

There is a fine line between growth and survival during the first few years of your new firm. Remember, there is no magic formula to help you make the transition between the introductory stage and the growth stage. Remain focused and true to your firm by constant attention and investment, and before you know it you will be in the growth stage.

Growth Stage

As in every business, if you are a good designer, it will not take long for the word to spread, and you will begin to receive and accept multiple commissions. The sheer number of projects to be handled, along with the deadlines imposed to get work done, will force you to consider delegating some tasks to others.

Deciding to Grow.   This is a critical time in your firm's life. You must make the decision to grow or not. By now, you probably have learned more about yourself than at any other time in your life. Can you manage others? Do you want to do it all? Can you delegate to others? Do you want to delegate? If you choose growth, start slowly. Don't let your ego get in the way and hire more staff than you really need.

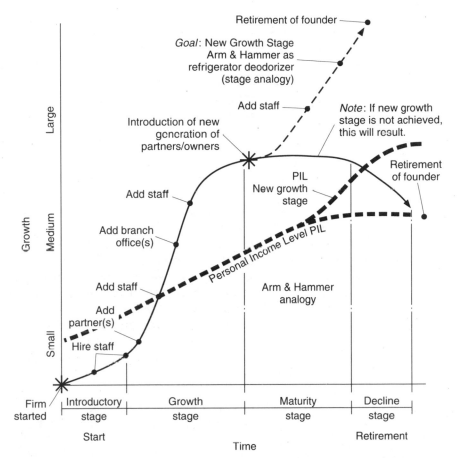

Design firm business cycles.

Remember, one person *can* do it all—but only by limiting intake and delivery. It is difficult to say no when potential clients show interest in you, providing you with a great opportunity to design a building for them. If you know yourself well and are sure you cannot say no, then growth is in your future. If you can say no, balance your schedule and keep demand in line with what it takes to maintain your own reputation. Then you can do it alone, with only yourself to criticize. This is the goal of many designers. However, you can also hire staff to help you design your buildings in the good times, then release them if necessary when the bad times come around. You will still be around to do the work.

Growth requires cash, so invest your profits back into the firm to add new equipment and staff. Banks love firms that grow, because growth devours cash! And guess who has the cash if your firm doesn't? When a firm experiences growth, profits are usually excellent, expansion begins, and issues such as relocation, upgrading firm image, and acquisitions and mergers become considerations.

One of the ways to address growth is by monitoring your firm's vital signs. When you are bringing in more business than you can possibly handle by yourself, it is time to get some design assistance. As noted in Chap. 12, there are only 168 hours in a week. You can physically work only so many hours. The workload will determine if your new assistant needs to be full or part time. Starting a person on a part-time basis is less risky. You won't have to provide benefits and other incentives, as you would for a full-time employee. Many designers with full-time staff jobs are looking for a "few extra bucks," and will be happy to assist you on weekends or evenings. You will be amazed at how this will help your business. You will be able to maintain the balance necessary and increase profitability!

The same holds true for the secretarial and accounting functions of the firm. If you are processing all the correspondence and specs, as well as handling all the bills and invoices, at some point you will become overwhelmed. These tasks can be done very cost-effectively by computer. However, if you are doing the tasks by hand, you will need help much sooner, and it will cost you more money in the long run.

The biggest bridge to cross as a designer facing growth is delegation. When do you let go and allow another to do the task? Remember, you are ultimately in charge and accountable. But you cannot do everything! You must give good instructions to those who will be supporting you.

Planning for Growth.   To understand business and achieve success in growth, you must understand the difference between controlled and explosive growth.

Controlled growth is the planned, intentional, logical, restrictive, organized expansion of a firm. It is calculated and monitored through regular checks and balances or reviews by you or management.

Explosive growth is the unplanned, unintentional, illogical, unrestrictive, unorganized expansion of a firm. It is reactive rather than proactive. It can be intoxicating as well as deadly. Explosive growth vaporizes cash! How many war stories do you know about firms that experienced explosive growth?

To be successful in the long run, you must think of your firm as an oak tree rather than a poplar. A poplar tree grows rapidly and is beautiful, but it can easily be destroyed by a bad wind storm. An oak tree is slow growing and deep rooted (the foundation is solid), and it will survive any storm, even an occasional lightning strike!

A *growth plan* is the development of the firm's master plan for its future growth and direction. The business plan outlines organization and tactics, the marketing plan outlines vision and strategies, and the growth plan outlines objectives such as these:

Specific targets for branch offices, number of employees, and equipment

Schedules associated with growth

Future needs for capital

Planned growth can be internal or external, or even a combination of both. Internal growth is developed with new equipment, new marketing materials, new spatial requirements, and new images for the firm. External growth develops through mergers and acquisitions, going public, or franchising the operations.

Growth, both internal and external, is a challenging issue to deal with. It can be exciting as well as demoralizing. However, remember that the challenges change daily and make the business world unpredictable. If all of us had the answers, how boring life would be. Plan for growth—and experience a whole new variety of challenges that will make your life more exciting in the future!

Maturity Stage

Every firm is different and reaches the third stage of business life, maturity, in a different time frame. In the maturity stage, the firm reaches its limit in size and performance. By now, the founder of the firm is older, more mature, and not as energetic and enthusiastic about the vitality and excitement of the firm's future. The founder is in a different phase of life: the kids have grown up, personal interests have changed, and the mind and body may not be as quick.

Experience and poise are the chief characteristics of the founder during this phase of the business. Growth becomes less important. Stability and experience begin to become more important than passion and living on the edge! However, these attributes may not be attractive to all potential clients. If growth is not maintained or rejuvenated by younger staff members, stagnation settles in, and it is only a matter of time before the firm begins to decline. Many designers cannot face the idea of others taking the reigns of the firm that they created. Some may sabotage the firm's future by stopping its growth and eventually closing the firm's doors.

Decline Stage

Ceasing to grow or refusing to change leads to decay and decline is the fourth stage of the business life cycle. The eventual result is the demise of the firm. But this need not always be the case.

A good example of decline stage "reversal" is Arm & Hammer baking soda. For years, the product was used for baking and cleaning, and as a toothpaste. Eventually, technical and marketing advancements in competitive products made baking soda lose market share. It was about to become extinct when some clever person decided that its odor-absorbing ability made it a wonderful refrigerator deodorant. Whoosh, baking soda roared back to become a stable household item in millions of refrigerators throughout the United States and the world!

Business needs to be flexible, to embrace change and develop fresh new ideas. Otherwise it will stagnate, decline, and die.

Monitoring Your Progress

Your New Firm's Vital Signs

Once you establish your goals and deal with your own way of managing fear, risk, and guilt, you must act much like a physician and monitor your new firm's vital signs steadily in order to keep it "alive."

The vital signs of the firm are its conscience. These signs raise questions in all areas of the firm, including administration, finance, marketing, and production.

Administration

How can I improve the firm with every situation that I encounter?

How can I be more productive?

Finance

How much money does it take to keep the doors open to this office every day?

How much money was received today?

What accounts receivable need attention today?

Did the invoices go out on the tenth?

CASH FLOW! CASH FLOW! CASH FLOW!

Marketing

Did I make two cold calls today?

Whom can I network with today, now?

Do any proposals need to be followed up?

How does the future workload look compared with the current workload?

Production

Am I billable 40 hours per week?

Am I managing my projects in the most effective way?

Am I understaffed?

Am I making my deadlines?

Am I happy with the firm's production tools?

Not only must you learn the vital signs, but you must become aware of when to micromanage and macromanage them. You must train yourself to address each sign, every day. If you pay too much attention to one, another will suffer. Once again, a critical balance must be maintained on a daily basis.

Besides monitoring your firm's vital signs internally, you can obtain outside assistance in evaluating the company and its progress through peer review and business owner support groups.

Peer Review

A peer review is having one or more successful practitioners, preferably not in your market area, evaluate the firm in administration, marketing, production, and finance. The review can help you keep track of your business cycle and progress. Learn from others.

The peer review team seeks to raise the level of a firm's professional practice by determining its objectives, policies, and procedures, and then examining its compliance with the objectives and procedures. The policies and technical competence of the firm are not evaluated by the peer reviewers.

To understand the policies, objectives, and procedures of a firm, the peer review team reviews the written documents furnished by the firm, ahead of time, probing into the following areas:

Management

Development and maintenance of technical competence

Management of projects

Human resources

Financial management

Business development

For smaller firms, the peer reviewers will interview the principal and key personnel if the firm's objectives and procedures are mentally established but not recorded.

The peer review is systematic and depends on communication and coordination. Its procedures, established and monitored by the American Consulting Engineers Council (ACEC), are as follows:

Firm requests peer review from ACEC.

Firm selects peer reviewers from list provided by ACEC.

ACEC coordinates schedules of reviewers and firm and establishes date of review.

ACEC gives list of materials required by firm to forward to reviewers.

Reviewers forward agreement of nondisclosure to firm.

Peer review is conducted.

Peer reviewers give verbal report at end of review to CEO.

Firm critiques the peer review and work of the reviewers.

The cost of the peer review is small compared with the benefit and value a firm will receive from having it. The firm pays for the travel and lodging expenses incurred by the review team along with an administrative fee and honoraria for the reviewers (currently $250 per reviewer per day). Member firms of the ACEC and AIA pay a little less.

The scale of the review is based on the size of the firm. In general, the following rules of thumb apply:

Firms with 1–15 staff	2 reviewers/1 day
Firms with 16–25 staff	2 reviewers/2 days
Firms with 26–60 staff	3 reviewers/2 days
Firms with more than 60 staff	3 or 4 reviewers/2 days

The problem many design firm principals have with a peer review is that they cannot bring themselves to open the firm and its management to criticism. As designers, we have been trained to accept constructive criticism on design, and we can review our employees' job performance according to our own criteria. However, having our abilities criticized as to how we run our firm—no way! It is important not to let this attitude turn into defensiveness. How can we become more effective unless we learn from others? None of us is perfect, especially in running a business!

A peer review gives you a snapshot of how your firm is doing. Check with your liability insurance carrier. Some carriers will reimburse you for the expense of conducting a peer review, because they recognize that you are trying to learn from the past and improve your practice, thus diminishing the risk of future liability claims.

A formal peer review should be a goal to achieve in the future. A review is generally not necessary for a young firm during the first few years. However, simply discussing the challenges and issues that you face day to day with colleagues and mentors is, to a degree, a minor peer review. Don't be afraid to share your concerns with friends and other colleagues. Designers often join the AIA in order to meet other practitioners who face the same issues. Many chapters have "small firm roundtables" and sole-proprietor groups.

Business Owner Support Groups

Business owner support groups provide another source of psychological help for coping with the current stage of your firm's business cycle. These groups are comprised of 6 to 10 individuals who meet once a month to discuss matters that affect their respective businesses.

For many, this is the way to go because the program is structured so that no two business owners who would be considered competitors are assigned to the same group. Another benefit is that all members of the group are total strangers. For many, this is the ultimate go-ahead to allow themselves to share their fears and secrets with others. For others, it takes a few sessions before trust and bonding develop so they can open up to the group.

Interestingly, no matter what line of work or profession you are in, the same business problems and issues arise. You may hear about someone else's problem and think that it cannot possibly affect your firm, but you never know. Also, having the opportunity to help others solve their business problems deepens your character and experience, and will help you deal more effectively with your own business problems.

Business owner support groups usually meet for a two-and-a-half-hour session, divided into three 45-minute segments. The first segment begins with the facilitator opening up the floor to discussion on business events that occurred in the past 30 days. Each participant summarizes, in 50 words or less, the trends and unique events that he or she has encountered. It is amazing how similar the reported issues are. The next segment is a "roundtable" in which one, two, or three issues are discussed by all. The final segment is usually focused on the vision quest of one business owner. The owner presents his or her background, the history of the company, its market and organization, and his or her vision of where the company is heading. The owner describes the problems he or she feels the firm will encounter as well as the firm's strengths and weaknesses. The group asks questions and critiques the presenter's information. Guidance is provided on many issues that the owner might have a difficult time discussing with a spouse, partner, or friend. Business is business, and owners understand owners.

Joining a group like this provides valuable feedback as well as a potential network of opportunities! Contact your local chamber of commerce to see if a business owner support group is established in your area.

Summary

The future of your firm is here, today, now. The fact is that no matter how experienced you are or how old your firm is, like every other business owner, you must *restart every day!* As with an automobile, you turn over the engine with the ignition and starter—every single morning.

Every new day brings fresh new challenges to face, requiring new solutions. These solutions may be based upon former ones (experience) or on advice from others. However, one thing is clear: No matter how mundane or repetitive things seem on the surface, every day is different. This is what is so exciting about operating your own firm. It never gets dull. It may get fatiguing, but it is never boring.

So if you are considering starting your own firm, what are you waiting for? Join the rest of us in the business arena who launch new firms every day! Learn to depend on your friends, your spouse, and your colleagues. Make this book your silent partner. Write in it, share its ideas, carry it with you, keep it in an accessible place!

This book comes with no guarantees. However, if you follow the suggestions made throughout its chapters, you stand a good chance of achieving success. Remember these rules of thumb:

Grow your contact network.

Market yourself to everyone and everything.

Learn to negotiate.

Learn how to sell yourself.

Subcontract with other designers to improve your profits.

Follow up on all marketing leads.

Rely on and trust your accountant, attorney, and bookkeeper.

Monitor your firm's vital signs.

Maintain the necessary critical balance in your life:

Approach your business fresh and confident.
Take time out to charge up your batteries.

Don't give up! You must not lose sight of success.

Maintain a sense of humor.

Learn to take risks.

Learn to manage fear, guilt, and success.

Remember to share your good experiences with your friends, colleagues, and spouse, because you will certainly be sharing the bad ones with them during your journey! Be considerate of them, because life without them would be impossible.

Set obtainable goals. Maintain your vision for your company, and above all be flexible in your practice. Learn to accept the bad events that you will inevitably encounter. In business as well as life, no one can fully appreciate the good without understanding and appreciating the bad.

Learn to accept that you will receive all the business that you *need*, not necessarily all the business that you *want*.

Learn from your mistakes as well as those of others. Take manageable risks, and exercise your business conscience in every single matter that you handle. Stay focused, passionate, and aggressive. Manage your fear, your clients, your partner(s), your employees, and most important, yourself!

One final note of hope is that when you are successful, living well will be the best revenge! Good luck!

Sample Design Proposal

June 1, 1994

Mr. & Mrs. Robert L. Smith
601 Crest Horn Road
Towson, Maryland Zip Code

Re: Residential addition to 601 Crest Horn Road

Dear Mr. and Mrs. Smith:

Apple Architecture, Inc. is pleased to present this proposal for professional architectural services to design and produce construction documents for the proposed great room/kitchen/bedroom addition to 601 Crest Horn Road in Towson.

Scope of Work

As discussed in our first meeting on Tuesday, May 26, 1993, it is our understanding that you plan to construct a new great room/kitchen/bedroom addition (approximately 900 square feet, on two levels) on the south side of your home.

Your hope is to connect the addition to the existing house across the entire 33-foot length of the south elevation and enclose the existing breezeway, which connects to the existing garage. Further, you desire to renovate/"modernize" the existing kitchen, upgrading the cabinetry, countertops, and appliances. Your plan is to construct the addition of wood frame with a crawl space in lieu of a basement. The exterior finish can be brick or siding, which will depend solely on the budget.

The great room is to "bring the outdoors inside," with the use of as much glass as possible to provide a view of the existing backyard. It is to be open to the existing living room and it is to have bookshelves but no fireplace. There is a desire to have a vaulted (cathedral) ceiling in the space.

The kitchen addition is to provide space for a dining table for four to six. It, like the great room, is to have a view of the backyard. The kitchen modernization is to include new appliances, cabinetry, and countertops, and is to be connected to the new eating area.

The new master bedroom is to be located on the addition's second floor. It is to have its own private bathroom, including water closet, double-bowl vanity, and tub/shower unit (or, if possible, a tub with separate shower). The bedroom is to be seventeen (17) feet by seventeen (17) feet minimum, in size. Sixteen (16) to twenty (20) lineal feet of closet space is to be provided. A secondary "back" stair is to be studied for inclusion in the project providing access to the area from the first level.

The new addition is to have its own HVAC system zone. Since the existing house has gas-fired heat only, it appears that a gas-fired heating and air conditioning system for the new addition is logical. Further, the goal for the project is to add a new air conditioning unit to the existing house HVAC system, utilizing the existing forced-air ductwork.

Finally, an outdoor wood deck is to be masterplanned off the rear of the house. At this time, the deck may be considered an alternate. (We will design, but not produce, construction documents for permit.)

Your hope is to build the two-storey addition and kitchen alteration for approximately $85,000 to $100,000 (900 square feet at $100 per square foot plus $10,000 for the kitchen upgrade). This figure does not include contingency fees, or furnishings.

Finally, we discussed a scope of work necessary to accomplish your project.

We have organized our services to accomplish the scope of work into the following five phases:

Phase I.	Field measurement and documentation of existing conditions
Phase II.	Conceptual design phase
Phase III.	Construction document phase
Phase IV.	Bid phase (optional)
Phase V.	Construction administration phase (optional)

Phase I. Documentation of Existing Conditions

Upon receipt of an approved, executed proposal, we will schedule a mutually agreeable time to visit your home and field measure the first floor, second floor, and basement. Further, we will photograph the interior as well as the exterior of the house to document the existing conditions. We estimate that we will need approximately one-half day to conduct this exercise.

After completion of our field survey, we will return to our office and draft the existing first floor, second floor, and basement floor plans. Additionally, we will draft the existing south (rear) and east and west (side) elevations. Upon completion, we will forward one copy of the drawings to you for your review.

Time frame   1 week

Fee $500 on an hourly, not-to-exceed basis

Phase II. Conceptual Design

Apple Architecture, Inc., will develop alternate conceptual floor plan designs based upon the scope of the project. Our documentation will include floor plans and a site plan for your review at one meeting in our office. The goal of our review meeting will be to refine the many ideas presented into one approved design. This approved concept will be refined into a final site plan, floor plan, and elevations to be presented at a final design review meeting in our office. The approved design will be presented to one or two contractors at a future meeting to confirm the conceptual budget for the addition.

Time frame   2 weeks

Fee $950 on an hourly, not-to-exceed basis

Phase III. Construction Documents

Upon approval of the conceptual design phase and conceptual design budget, we will proceed with the construction document phase, producing construction drawings and specifications for building permit applications and for the basis of construction.

At this time, we have figured an allowance of time (60 to 80 hours) to produce the necessary construction documents. We felt that quoting the range was the most fair to you and our firm. We shall endeavor to conduct our services within this range of time.

Time frame   4 weeks

Fee $2400 to $3200 on an hourly, not-to-
                             exceed basis

Phase IV. Bid/Negotiation Phase (Optional)

Upon completion of the construction document phase, we can assist you on the coordination of pricing for the addition and answer any questions that the contractors may have concerning the design and drawings. Services could be for a one-time exercise with up to five (5) bidders.

Time frame   3 weeks

Fee $750 on an hourly, not-to-exceed basis

Phase V. Construction Administration (Optional)

We estimate that your addition will have a construction time frame of approximately 4 to 6 months. Experience tells us that we may average approximately 2 hours per week during that 16 to 26 week period, answering questions, making 8 site visits, developing one punch list walk-through, one final walk-through, and reviewing submittals for your project. Therefore, we recommend a time allowance in which we will bill you by the hour, not to exceed 50 hours on construction administration time for our architectural staff.

Time frame   16 to 26 weeks

Fee $2500 on an hourly, not-to-exceed basis

Summary of Fees

Phase I.   Document existing conditions $ 500

Phase II. Conceptual design   950

Phase III. Construction documents   2400 to 3200

  Subtotal $3850 to $4650

                                                             (On an hourly, not-to-
                                                             exceed basis)

Optional services

Phase IV. Bid/Negotiation	$ 750
Phase V. Construction administration	2500

(On an hourly, not-to-exceed basis)

Exclusions

Please note that the above quoted figures do not include any of the following:

Professional land survey

Civil engineering design

Mechanical, electrical, plumbing engineering design

Landscape architecture design (conceptual patio design is included in the proposal)

Structural engineering of special conditions or retaining-wall design

Cost estimating

Kitchen design

Appliance selection

Special stereo and security system selection

Furniture inventory and selection

Accessory and artwork selection

Interior design services

Permit filing or expediting fees with Baltimore County

Reimbursable Expenses

Reimbursable expenses such as printing, photography, long distance communications, application and filing of building permit, soil borings, etc., will be provided on an as-needed basis and will be billed monthly with a 15 percent administrative charge.

Additional Services

Should additional services be requested by you due to a change in scope of the services required, we will proceed with said services upon your written approval, and invoice on an hourly basis based on the following hourly rates:

Principal	$95
Managing architect	75
Staff architect	45
Staff Designer	35
Drafter	30
Administrative	25
Managing interior designer	55

Miscellaneous Provisions

Invoices will be sent monthly with payment due within 30 days of receipt. Should the production effort be interrupted due to late receipt of payments, it will be necessary to adjust the schedule. Interest will be billed at the rate of 1.5 percent per month on the balance outstanding, 30 days after the date of the invoice, and will be added and compounded monthly.

We specifically reserve the right to suspend or terminate our services if payment is not received within the time period specified.

We reserve the right to withhold plans and documents from the review, signature, or distribution process, if account is not currently paid.

This proposal will remain in effect for a period of not less than one year from the effective date hereof. At that time, we reserve the right to revise our rates in accordance with changes in our operating costs. Written notification will be given 30 days prior to the effective date of any such change in rates.

Please advise as soon as possible the status of our proposal so that we may schedule our work accordingly.

If this proposal is satisfactory, please sign where indicated and return the enclosed copy as your acceptance of its terms and as our authorization to proceed.

As always, should you have any questions concerning any of the above information, please feel free to contact me. It was a pleasure meeting with you to discuss various issues relating to your needs. We look forward to working with you on your challenging project.

Regards,

George Macintosh Apple III, AIA
President
Apple Architecture, Inc.

Acceptance

The proposed description of professional services and terms are satisfactory and are hereby accepted. Authorization to proceed with the work is granted.

The terms of this proposal shall be null and void if not accepted within 60 days.

Name_____

Date_____

Appendix **B**

Glossary of
Accounting Terms

Accounting: The recording and reporting of all business transactions for use in making future business decisions.

Accounting Cycle: Source documents, journal, ledger, trial balance, adjustments (accruals), adjusted trial balance, income statement, balance sheet, closing entries, and postclosing trial balance.

Accounting Equation: Assets = liabilities + owner's equity.

Accounting Period: The length of time for which an income statement is customarily prepared.

Accounts Payable: An amount (liability) owed to a creditor (consultant, blueprinter, vendor, etc.), generally on an open account.

Accounts Receivable: A claim (asset) against a debtor (client) for services performed.

Accrual Basis: The practice of recording a revenue or expense transaction (accounts receivable or accounts payable) during the accounting period in which it occurs rather than in the period when actual payment is made or recognized.

Asset: Anything of monetary (cash) value owned by a business (furniture, equipment, etc.).

Audit: Any inspection by a third person of accounting records involving analysis, testing, proof, and confirmation.

Balance Sheet: A statement showing the status of all assets, liabilities, and owner's equity on a specific date.

Book Value: The value of a stock determined from a company's records by adding all assets (excluding goodwill) and then deducting all debts and other liabilities plus the liquidation price of any preferred issues. The sum arrived at is divided by the number of common shares outstanding and the result is book value per common share.

Bookkeeping: The recording of financial data from source documents to journals and ledgers.

Capital: The owner's investment in a business; not synonymous with cash. Capital can include cash, equipment, furniture, or any asset.

Cash: Money (currency and coins), money orders, bank deposits, and bank credit card balances; the first asset listed on the balance sheet.

Cash Basis: The practice of recording income and expenses only when cash is actually received or paid out.

Cash Discount: The amount, usually a percentage (%), that a vendor will deduct from the total price for prompt payment.

Creditor: An entity that loans or gives credit in a business transaction.

Depreciation: The monetary loss in service, capacity, or utility from a fixed asset (car, computer, furniture, etc.); a type of business expense.

Expense: A cost of operating a business (telephone, salaries, rent, letterhead, business cards, etc.); also called *overhead*.

General Ledger: The book of original bookkeeping entries, in which data from source documents is first recorded.

Gross Margin: Total fees minus the cost of services sold; also called *markup*.

Income Statement: A statement providing information about revenue and expenses over a specific period of time.

Liability: An obligation of a business to pay a debt (account payable, note payable, etc.) to a creditor.

Liquidity: The ability of a business to readily convert all accounts receivable and other assets into cash.

Note: An unconditional written promise to pay a certain sum of money.

Owner's Equity: The net worth of the business, defined as capital + income – expenses.

Payroll: A record showing the wages and salaries earned by employees along with various deductions (for withholding taxes, insurance, retirement plans, etc.).

Petty Cash: A small amount of cash on hand, used for minor disbursements, when payment by check is impractical.

Posting: The process of recording information from a journal to the general ledger.

Prepaid Expenses: Current assets that become expenses as they are used; supplies are an example.

Retained Earnings: An accumulation of earnings which have not been paid out to stockholders in a corporation.

Return on Investment: The ratio of profits to net worth or stockholders' equity.

Revenue: Any source of income for a business.

Transaction: Any business activity involving an exchange of money values.

Trial Balance: A list of all accounts proving the ledger; debits must equal credits.

Appendix C

Glossary of Legal Terms

Affidavit: A sworn statement in writing.

Affirmative Action: A court-ordered requirement that employers who in the court's judgment have practiced job discrimination against a minority in the past extend favorable treatment to minority members in the work force.

Annual Percentage Rate (APR): The true interest rate, arrived at by taking into consideration all finance charges.

Arbitration: The hearing and determination of a civil dispute by a person or persons chosen or approved by both parties.

Capital Stock: The total stock issued by a corporation.

Chapter 7: A section of the Federal Bankruptcy Act which grants debtors the right to clear themselves of debt by paying a percentage or nothing of what they owe.

Chapter 13: A section of the Federal Bankruptcy Act which grants debtors the right to pay off all or part of their debts on an easy payment plan under protection of the court.

Contract: An agreement upon sufficient consideration to do or not to do a particular act.

Corporation: A form of business regarded by law as a person, distinct from the persons who own it; owners are therefore not responsible for the debts of the corporation.

Defendant: The person against whom a legal action is brought.

General Partnership: A partnership in which each member is responsible for the acts of the other partners and for all partnership debts.

Goodwill: An intangible asset arising from the reputation of a business and its relations with its customers; distinct from the value of business stock and other tangible assets.

Lien: A legal claim against property, usually as a result of debt.

Limited Partnership: A partnership in which the liability of some of the members (limited partners) is restricted to the amount of their respective investments.

Litigation: A method of resolving disputes through a legal contest carried out by judicial process.

Mediation: A method of intervening in a civil dispute to promote reconciliation, compromise, or settlement; solutions may or may not be accepted by the contending parties.

Negligence: Failure to exercise reasonable care, resulting in accidental injury to another person or persons.

Partnership: An agreement of two or more parties to conduct an unincorporated business.

Plaintiff: A person who brings a lawsuit or civil action to a court, the complaining person.

Preferred Stock: Stock that is superior to common stock with respect to dividends and often to asset sharing in the event of liquidation.

Sole Proprietorship: An unincorporated business with a single owner.

Statute: A law enacted by a legislature and expressed in a formal document.

Statutory Law: A body of law enacted by a legislature.

Stock: The ownership shares of a corporation authorized by its articles of incorporation, including both common and preferred stock.

Stockholder: A holder or owner of stock in a corporation.

Tort: A wrongful act resulting in damage or injury, often willfully or negligently performed, for which a civil suit can be brought.

Appendix D
Glossary of Banking Terms

Amortization: The gradual reduction of debt by means of equal periodic payments sufficient to meet current interest and liquidate the debt at maturity.

Appreciation: The increase in value of an asset in excess of its depreciable cost as a result of economic and other conditions; distinguished from increases in value arising from improvements or additions to the asset.

Average Daily Balance: The average amount of money that a customer keeps on deposit, determined by adding the daily balances of an account for a given length of time and dividing the total by the number of days.

Bad Debts: Amounts due on open accounts receivable that have proved uncollectible.

Bank Reconciliation: Verification of a bank statement balance and the depositor's checkbook balance.

Depreciation: The amount of expense charged against business earnings in order to write off the cost of a plant or machine over its useful life, giving consideration to wear and tear, obsolescence, and salvage. Under straight-line depreciation, the expense is assumed to be incurred in equal amounts in each business year over the life of the asset. Under accelerated depreciation, the expense is assumed to be incurred in decreasing amounts in each business year over the life of the asset.

Line of Credit: An agreement between a bank and a company whereby the bank lends the company funds up to a previously agreed upon maximum amount. A line of credit is used by business for future commitments and purchases in times of growth or slow cash flow.

Liquidity: The solvency of a business, or the degree to which its assets can readily be converted into cash without loss.

Long-Term Debt: An obligation that will not become due for at least one year.

Mortgage: A written obligation to pay a debt over time, with the underlying asset pledged as security.

Nonforfeiture option: One of the choices available if the policyholder discontinues premium payments on a policy with a cash value. It may be taken in liquid cash, or as extended term insurance, or as reduced, paid-up insurance.

Retained Earnings: An accumulation of earnings which have not been paid out to stockholders.

Secured Loan: A loan that is secured by marketable securities or other marketable valuables.

Short-term Debt: An obligation which will be due in full within a one-year time frame.

Term Loan: A long-term loan with a life of up to 10 years.

Unsecured Loan: A loan that is not secured by a marketable security or asset.

Appendix **E**

Glossary of Insurance Terms

Accumulation Period: A specified length of time during which the insured must incur eligible medical expenses at least equal to the deductible amount to establish a benefit period under a medical policy.

Actuary: A trained professional in the technical aspects of insurance mathematics (calculations of premiums, reserves, annuities, and other values).

Adjustable Life Insurance: An insurance plan that allows the policyholder to change certain terms: raise or lower the face value of the policy, increase or decrease the premium, and lengthen or shorten the protection period.

Age Limits: Established minimum and maximum ages for which an insurance company will not accept applications or renew policies.

Agent: An insurance company representative licensed by the state who solicits and sells insurance and services claims made by policyholders.

Aggregate Indemnity: The maximum dollar amount that may be collected for any disability or period of disability under an insurance policy.

Allocated Benefits: Benefits for which the maximum amount payable for specific services is itemized in the contract.

Beneficiary: The person designated or provided for by the policy terms to receive the benefits of the policy.

Benefits: The amount paid by the insurance company to a claimant or beneficiary under coverage.

Broker: An insurance solicitor licensed by a state who places business with a variety of insurance companies.

Business Insurance: An insurance policy that provides coverage of benefits to a business rather than an individual. It is issued to indemnify a business for loss or services when a key employee or a partner becomes disabled.

Business Life Insurance: Insurance purchased by a business on the life of a member of the firm. It is purchased to protect the surviving owners or partners from loss of services when a key employee or partner dies.

Cash Surrender Value: The amount available in cash upon voluntary termination of a policy by its owner, before the policy becomes payable by death or maturity.

Certificate of Insurance: A statement of coverage issued to an individual insured under a group insurance contract, outlining the insurance benefits and principal provisions applicable to the member.

Claim: Notification to an insurance company that payment of an amount is being sought under the terms of a particular policy.

Convertible Term Insurance: Term insurance which can be exchanged, at the policyholder's option and without evidence of insurability, for another plan of insurance.

Credit Life Insurance: Term life insurance issued through a lender to cover payment of a loan in the case of death.

Deductible: The amount of covered charges that must be paid by the policyholder before benefits can be realized from the insurance company.

Deposit Term Insurance: A form of term insurance in which the first-year premium is larger than subsequent premiums.

Disability: A partial or total physical or mental handicap resulting from sickness or injury.

Disability Benefit: A policy feature providing for waiver of premium, and sometimes payment of monthly income, if the policyholder becomes totally and permanently disabled.

Disability Income Insurance: A form of insurance that provides payments to replace income when the policyholder becomes disabled as a result of illness or injury.

Dividend: A return on part of a premium to a policyholder that reflects the difference between the actual premium charged and a combination of the insurance company's actual mortality, expense, and investment experience.

Double Indemnity: A policy provision that doubles payment of a designated benefit when certain kinds of fatal accidents occur.

Duplication of Benefits: The overlapping or identical coverage of the same policyholder under two or more health plans.

Effective Date: The date on which coverage under an insurance policy begins.

Eligibility Date: The date on which an individual or a particular group becomes eligible to apply for insurance under a group life or health insurance plan.

Eligibility Period: A specified length of time following the eligibility date during which an individual or a particular group will remain eligible to apply for insurance under a group life or health insurance policy without evidence of insurability.

Eligible Employees: Members of a group who have met the eligibility requirements under a group life or health plan.

Elimination Period: A period of time between the period of disability and the start of disability income insurance benefits, during which no benefits are payable.

Evidence of Insurability: Any statement of proof of a person's physical condition and/or other factual information affecting the individual's eligibility for insurance.

Exclusions: Specific conditions or circumstances listed in the policy for which no benefit payments will be provided.

Extended Term Insurance: A form of insurance, available as a nonforfeiture option, in which the original amount of insurance is provided for a limited period of time.

Grace Period: A period following the premium date during which an overdue premium may be paid without penalty.

Group Life Insurance: Life insurance provided on a group of people under a master policy.

Health Insurance: Insurance protection that provides payment of benefits for covered sickness or injury.

Health Maintenance Organization (HMO): An organization that provides a wide range of health-care services for a specified group at a fixed periodic payment.

Hospital Expense Insurance: Protection against the cost of hospital care resulting from the illness or injury of the policyholder.

Insurance: Protection by written contract (policy) against hazards.

Key Person Health Insurance: An individual or group insurance policy designed to protect a business against loss of income resulting from the disability of a key employee.

Level Premium: A premium that remains unchanged throughout the life of a policy.

Level Premium Life Insurance: A life insurance policy in which the premium remains the same from year to year.

Lifetime Disability Benefit: A benefit to help replace income lost by a policyholder for as long as he or she is totally disabled—even for a lifetime.

Long-Term Disability Income Insurance: Insurance issued to an employer group or individual to provide for replacement of a portion of an employee's earned income lost as a result of serious and prolonged illness or injury.

Major Medical Insurance: Health insurance to cover the expenses of major illness and injury.

Ordinary Life Insurance: Life insurance issued in amounts of $1000 or more, with premiums payable on an annual, semiannual, quarterly, or monthly basis.

Overhead Insurance: A type of short-term disability income insurance that reimburses the insured person for specified, fixed monthly expenses, that are normal and customary in the operation of a business.

Paid-up Insurance: Insurance on which all required premiums have been paid.

Permanent Life Insurance: Insurance that accrues in cash value, such as whole life insurance or an endowment.

Policy Loan: A loan made by the insurance company to the policyholder on the security of the cash value of the policy.

Policyholder: The person, partnership, or corporation that owns the insurance policy.

Premium: The payment that the policyholder agrees to make to keep an insurance policy in force.

Preexisting Condition: A physical and/or mental condition of an insured policyholder that first manifested itself prior to issuance of the policy or that existed and was given treatment prior to issuance.

Preferred Provider Organization (PPO): A group of medical-care providers that furnish services to a group at lower than usual fees in exchange for an agreement guaranteeing prompt payment and a certain volume of patients.

Renewal: Continuation of coverage beyond the original agreement by the policyholder's acceptance of the premium for a new policy term.

Renewable Term Insurance: Term insurance that can be renewed at the end of a term at the option of the policyholder.

Rider: A special policy provision or group of provisions added to a policy to expand or limit the benefits otherwise payable.

Self-Insurance: A program for providing group insurance with benefits financed entirely by the employer in place of purchasing coverage from commercial insurance companies.

Short-Term Disability Income Insurance: Insurance that pays benefits to a disabled policyholder for a specified period of time, usually not exceeding two years.

Straight Life Insurance: Whole life insurance in which premiums are payable for the life of the policyholder.

Term Insurance: Life insurance that has no cash value unless the policyholder dies within a specified time period; benefits are payable only to the beneficiary.

Third-Party Administrator: A business that administrates group health insurance plans for associations and clubs.

Universal Life Insurance: A flexible-premium life insurance policy under which the policyholder may change the death benefit from time to time and vary the amount or timing of premium payments.

Variable Life Insurance: Life insurance under which the benefit relates to the value of assets behind the contract at the time the benefit is paid.

Waiting Period: The length of time an employee must wait to gain insurance coverage from an employer.

Whole Life Insurance: Life insurance that develops a cash value, which may be drawn upon or cashed out by the policyholder (e.g., for retirement purposes) or paid out to a beneficiary at the death of the policyholder.

Workers' Compensation: Insurance to pay benefits and furnish care to employees injured on the job or to compensate dependents of employees killed on the job.

Appendix **F**

References

Allen, Edward. *Architect's Studio Companion: Simplified Technical Guidelines for Preliminary Design.* New York: John Wiley, 1989.

Birnberg & Associates. *Financial Management for Small Design Firms.* Chicago, IL: Birnberg & Associates, 1985.

Birnberg & Associates. *Small Design Firm Marketing Manual.* Chicago, IL: Birnberg & Associates, 1985.

Birnberg, Howard G. *Improving Productivity in Small Design Firms.* Chicago, IL: Birnberg & Associates, 1990.

Coxe, Weld, Hon. AIA. *Success Strategies for Design Professionals.* New York: McGraw-Hill, 1987.

Edmunds, Jane C. *Public Relations for Small Design Firms.* Chicago, IL: Birnberg & Associates, 1988.

Franklin, James R., AIA. *Current Practices in Small Firm Management: An Architect's Notebook.* Washington, DC: American Institute of Architects, 1990.

Franklin, James R., AIA. *How to Start Your Own Firm Kit,* accompanying *Current Practices in Small Firm Management: An Architect's Notebook.* Washington, DC: American Institute of Architects.

Getz, Lowell, CPA. *Business Management in the Smaller Design Firm: Practical Techniques for Architects, Engineers, and Interior Designers.* Newton, MA: Practice Management Associates, 1986.

Getz, Lowell, CPA, and Frank Stasiowski, AIA. *Financial Management for the Design Professional.* New York: Whitney Library of Design, 1984.

Haviland, David, ed. *Architect's Handbook of Professional Practice.* 11th ed; 4 vols. Washington, DC: American Institute of Architects, 1988. See chapter 1.9, "Organization and Management," by Hugh Hochberg.

Haviland, David. *Managing Architectural Projects: The Project Management Manual.* 4 vols. Washington, DC: American Institute of Architects, 1984.

Kaderland, Norman. *Designing Your Practice: A Principal's Guide to Creating and Managing a Design Practice.* New York: McGraw-Hill, 1991.

Morgan, Jim. *Marketing for the Small Design Firm.* New York: Whitney Library of Design, 1984.

Stasiowski, Frank A., AIA. *Staying Small Successfully: A Guide for Architects, Engineers, and Design Professionals*. New York: John Wiley, 1991.

Stitt, Fred A., ed. *Design Office Management Handbook*. Santa Monica, CA: Arts and Architecture Press, 1982.

Whitmyer, Salli Rasberry, and Michael Phillips. *Running a One-Person Business*. Berkeley, CA: Ten Speed Press, 1989.

Index

About the Author

Albert W. Rubeling, Jr., FAIA, is the principal and owner of Rubeling & Associates, Inc., an architectural and interior design firm based in Towson, Maryland. He currently sits on the Board of Directors of the American Institute of Architects (AIA), as the Middle Atlantic Regional Director. Mr. Rubeling has long been active in the AIA committees on intern training and firm practice. He obtained his Bachelor of Architecture from the University of Maryland and is licensed to practice in 13 states. He started his own firm in 1981.